Aaron,

Happy Birthday!

This is a good book
to read and be aware
of. Tom Daschle will
be the next Secretary
of Health and Human
Service (DHHS).

Love,
Dad

CRITICAL

Also by Senator Tom Daschle

*Like No Other Time: The 107th Congress
and the Two Years that Changed America*
(with Michael D'Orso)

CRITICAL

What We Can Do About the Health-Care Crisis

Senator Tom Daschle

with SCOTT S. GREENBERGER
and JEANNE M. LAMBREW

Thomas Dunne Books ☎ St. Martin's Press

NEW YORK

To my grandchildren,
Henry, Ava, Benjamin, and Truman,
with heartfelt hope that each
will soon benefit from a new, high-value,
and universal health-care system

THOMAS DUNNE BOOKS.
An imprint of St. Martin's Press.

CRITICAL. Copyright © 2008 by Tom Daschle.
All rights reserved. Printed in the United States of America.
No part of this book may be used or reproduced in any manner whatsoever
without written permission except in the case of brief quotations
embodied in critical articles or reviews. For information, address St. Martin's Press,
175 Fifth Avenue, New York, N.Y. 10010.

www.thomasdunnebooks.com
www.stmartins.com

Library of Congress Cataloging-in-Publication Data are available upon request.

ISBN-13: 978-0-312-38301-5
ISBN-10: 0-312-38301-0

First Edition: February 2008

3 5 7 9 10 8 6 4 2

Contents

Acknowledgments

Health policy has been something on which I have worked for many years. In many respects, this book represents the culmination of that work to date. I have long felt that there is no more important issue facing our country than reform of our health-care system.

My sincere hope is that this work may help move us closer to the day when our system can reflect the greatness of our people by providing every American with health care of high value. And while I have studied the issue for nearly two decades, as with most books, the writing of it can be as much as or more of a learning experience for the author as it is for the reader. With research and intense discussion comes better understanding. This has been such an experience for me and, I trust, for our team.

As with all of my life, I want to thank my wife, Linda, for her constant support and tolerance. For a quarter century she has been there at every turn, in victory, defeat, and each new endeavor. That is true with this book, as it has been with virtually everything I have ever done.

I am deeply grateful for all of the extraordinary work of my colleague on this project, Jeanne Lambrew. Her wisdom, experience, and vision for a new system is evident on virtually every page. This has been a truly gratifying and enjoyable effort, thanks largely to Jeanne. I thank her profusely for her partnership and her constant guidance and support.

I also want to acknowledge Scott Greenberger, a most gifted writer. It has been my true pleasure to work with him as we put our ideas and research to paper. His responsiveness and ability to help us capture the essence of the book succinctly and, we hope, successfully has significantly improved our ability to recount the history of the health-reform movement and our ideas for a new health paradigm. I thank Scott for his remarkable contribution of research, writing, and guidance from start to finish.

I must certainly express my heartfelt thanks also to Denis McDonough for his extraordinary assistance with every aspect of this book. His wise counsel and superb organizational skills were of immense value throughout its writing. I doubt we could have succeeded without him. This is a far better book because of his contribution.

I also would like to thank John Podesta for his support for this project in concert with the Center for American Progress. His early willingness to provide support was instrumental at a critical moment in launching the effort. It is my great pleasure to work with him.

Meredith King was also extremely helpful. Her research and support contributed substantially to the accuracy and credibility of the information found on these pages. I am particularly grateful for all the help of my staff: Nancy Hogan, Lindsey Dorneman, and Jody Bennett. Their constant presence, professionalism, and dedication has provided me with immense support and assistance.

I am grateful to a number of friends and colleagues who helped us immensely as we worked to recount our health-care experiences over the past two decades. Chris Jennings, Rima Cohen, and David Nexon would be some of the first people in the room I would choose to design a new health-care system. I also want to acknowledge Dr. Jerry Grossman, who shares my passion for health reform and has spent his life dedicated to improving our country's health-care system.

I especially appreciate the support and commitment given to me by Thomas Dunne at St. Martin's Press. He has supported this project from the very beginning and has been critical in bringing the book to publication. Every writer should have the luxury of having such publisher support.

That must also be said of Victoria Skurnick, our agent and original advocate. I thank her for believing in this project and helping others to believe in it, too.

Someone once said that glory is not never failing, but getting up each time after you fail. I have thought about that little bit of wisdom many times in my life. Perhaps it applies to our efforts to reform health care in the United States, too. For nearly a century, our efforts have failed. But perhaps our glory will be realized one day for getting up each time to try again. We will get up. We will try again.

And one day, we will win.

Introduction

Some years ago, the president of the United States stood before Congress and proclaimed that it was time to guarantee health care to every American. "Millions of our citizens do not now have a full measure of opportunity to achieve and enjoy good health. Millions do not now have protection or security against the economic effects of sickness. The time has arrived for action to help them attain that opportunity and that protection," said the president, a Democrat. He continued: "People with low or moderate incomes do not get the same medical attention as those with high incomes. The poor have more sickness, but they get less medical care. People who live in rural areas do not get the same amount or quality of medical attention as those who live in our cities."

President Bill Clinton might have uttered those words in 1993, but he didn't. In fact, the presidential speech excerpted above predated President Clinton and his ill-fated attempt at health-care reform by nearly a half-century. The quote belongs to President Harry Truman, and it was part of a speech Truman delivered to a joint session of Congress in 1945 to promote his own, doomed plan to guarantee health care to every American. Like Clinton, Truman had reason to be confident. His fellow Democrats controlled both houses of Congress, and polls showed that Americans were anxious about the high cost of health care and eager for change. But both presidents underestimated the strength of the forces arrayed against them. Special-interest lobbyists—led by doctors in Truman's time, and insurance companies in Clinton's—fanned the public's fear that government bureaucrats would come between doctors and patients. Additionally, public support had greater breadth than depth. Both presidents' health-care plans became bogged down in Congress. And when the Republicans triumphed in the subsequent midterm elections in 1946 and 1994, health-care reform was effectively dead. "I have had some bitter disappointments as president, but the one that troubled me most, in a personal way, has been the failure to defeat the organized opposition to a national compulsory health insurance plan," Truman wrote in his memoirs.

Sixty years and four attempts later, the depressing picture that Truman painted is still an accurate if understated portrait of our broken health-care system. Millions of Americans go without medical care because they can't afford it, and many others are mired in debt because they can't pay their medical bills. It's hard to think of another public policy problem that has lingered, mostly unaddressed, for so long. Why have we failed to solve a problem that is such a high priority for so many citizens? The answer, I believe, is rooted in the complexity of the health-care issue, the limitations of our political system, and the power of the interest groups—doctors, hospitals, insurers, drug companies, researchers, and even patient advocates—that have a direct stake in it.

How can we cut through this Gordian knot? I believe that the only way to solve the health-care crisis is to change the way that we approach the challenge. In this book, I propose a Federal Health Board, modeled loosely on the Federal Reserve System, to do so. It would create a public framework for a largely private health-care delivery system. Its main job would be to develop the standards and structure for a health system that ensures accessible, affordable, and high-quality care. These standards would apply to federal health programs and contractors and serve as a model for private insurers. The federal government, through programs like Medicare, Medicaid, and the Veterans Health Administration, provides health care to roughly 100 million people. But these programs have disparate benefits, quality standards, and success in cost containment. If an independent board created a single set of standards for all of these programs, it would exert tremendous influence on every other provider and payer, even those in the private sector.

Like the Federal Reserve, the Federal Health Board would be composed of highly independent experts insulated from politics. Congress and the White House would relinquish some of their health-policy decisions to it. For example, a shift to a more effective drug or service could be accomplished without an act of Congress or White House political support. This power is not small, and delegation rightly raises concerns. But imagine the outcomes if Congress revoked the Fed's power to set interest rates and instead took it upon itself to enact them each quarter. It would be a disaster—no less so than the results of decades of mismanagement of our health system.

The Federal Health Board I propose would not solve all our health-care problems. Our system is fundamentally broken, and decades of failed incremental measures have proven that we need a comprehensive approach to fix it. Undeniably, it will be difficult to change a system that accounts for more than 16 percent of our economy—and has a direct impact on every man, woman, and child in the United States. Moving from the current system to one that guarantees universal coverage will force us to wade into a myriad of complicated details—details that disaffected people, parties, or interest groups can seize upon to derail the entire effort. Nevertheless, the problem is not intractable. With the right approach, including a Federal Health Board, it can be solved.

Part One

THE CRISIS

Stories Behind the Statistics

BEFORE EXPLORING MY idea in detail, it's worthwhile to review the current state of affairs. By almost any measure, the situation is grim. We like to boast that we have the highest standard of living in the world, and yet at the dawn of the twenty-first century, we are the only industrialized nation that does not guarantee necessary health care to all of its citizens. It is stunning and shameful. There are about 47 million Americans without health insurance, and researchers have estimated that about four-fifths of them are either employed or members of a family with an employed adult.[1] An additional 16 million people are "underinsured," or have coverage that would not protect them from catastrophic medical expenses.[2] Simply put, an increasing number of Americans lack health insurance because they—and their employers—just can't afford it.

Only 65 percent of people earning less than $10 an hour are offered health insurance at work. Furthermore, as health-care costs have exploded, many employers who offer coverage have reduced the portion of the premiums they cover. As a result, many working people can't afford coverage even when it is made available to them. Other firms are eliminating coverage for prescription drugs, dental care, vision care, and care of dependents.[3] And it isn't just low-wage workers or the unemployed who are in danger: Statistics show that more middle-class people—families with annual incomes of $50,000 or more—are joining the ranks of the uninsured. Today, 18 million of the roughly 47 million people without insurance have family incomes that exceed $50,000.[4]

Vicki H. Readling, a fifty-year-old real estate agent and breast cancer survivor from Salisbury, North Carolina, knows this all too well. Real estate agents are independent contractors, so Readling doesn't have medical coverage through an employer. She earned about $60,000 in 2006, a solidly middle-class salary in the Piedmont region of her state. But because of her medical history, the only policy Readling could find on the individual insurance market would have cost her more than $27,000 a year, far more than she could afford. She delays visits to the doctor and makes her $300-a-month cancer medication last longer by taking it only three or four times a week instead of every day. "I really try to stay away from the doctor because I am so scared of what everything will cost," Readling said in an interview with *The New York Times*. "Why am I being punished? I just don't understand how I could have fallen through this horrible, horrible crack."[5]

More than 16 percent of our economy, or $2 trillion, is spent on health care. On a per person basis, Americans spent more than $6,100 on medical care in 2004, more than twice the industrial world's average and about 50 percent more than the next most expensive country, Switzerland.[6] This disparity is even more striking when one considers that in every other industrialized country, every citizen is covered. Between 2000 and 2007, U.S. health premiums have risen 98 percent, while wages have increased by only 23 percent. The average family health insurance policy now costs more than the earnings of a full-time, minimum-wage worker.[7] No wonder medical bills are the leading cause of bankruptcy in the United States, accounting for about half of them. Incredibly, one fifth of working-age Americans—both insured and uninsured—have medical debt they are paying off over time. More than two-fifths of these people owe $2,000 or more.[8]

Representing South Dakota, where incomes are lower than in most other states, I encountered many families who were struggling to pay their medical bills. One woman who made an especially vivid impression on me was Donna S. Smith, one of the thousands of Americans who literally have been driven to bankruptcy by our health-care system. Smith isn't a deadbeat or a slacker—far from it. During the early years of her marriage, she stayed at home to care for her six children while her husband Larry worked as a machinist. When their youngest child was two, Donna decided to go back to work.

At thirty-one, discouraged by a series of minimum-wage jobs, she enrolled in college courses while still working full-time as a bank teller. Eventually she earned a bachelor's degree from Colorado College in Colorado Springs—graduating cum laude and Phi Beta Kappa. I met her when she was working as a journalist for one of our South Dakota newspapers.

Donna and Larry always had health insurance for themselves and their children—they even carried disability insurance—but that didn't shield them from financial ruin once they encountered serious health problems. After Larry developed coronary artery disease in the early 1990s, he could no longer work as a machinist. Instead, he did light maintenance work, delivered pizza, and toiled as a cashier, earning far less than he had before.

The financial pressure mounted after Donna was diagnosed with uterine cancer in 1999. Just weeks after undergoing surgery, she returned to her job caring for disabled children in a group home because she desperately needed the income, and she feared that if she stayed away too long she'd lose the job and the health coverage that went with it. She wore an abdominal brace and a back belt to protect her incision site, but those precautions didn't prevent her from developing an abdominal hernia, and she had to have surgery again in the summer of 2000.

Donna recovered, but the family's premium payments, drug costs, and co-payments went through the roof. By 2003, their monthly medical expenses were more than $1,000, and Larry's continuing health problems frequently forced him to miss work. The Smiths did what they could to stay afloat. They bought food and other household goods on credit, and borrowed money against their cars. When things got truly desperate, they visited a local food pantry and tapped family and friends for help.

They sold their house, but the sale netted them a paltry $8,000. In the spring of 2004, Larry lost his job at a casino because he could no longer do any heavy lifting. With bill collectors practically beating down their door, the Smiths declared bankruptcy. Two years later, the couple was forced to move in with their grown daughter and her family in Denver. "The life we worked so hard to build and the life we fought to save was lost. We had failed. The health-care system had crushed us," Donna Smith told House members during a hearing held in July 2007. After telling her story, Smith chastised the lawmakers for failing to do something about our broken health-care system.

> I am so angry with you. I lived the American dream as my father taught me and as his father taught him. I worked, I educated myself, I voted, I bought a home and then moved up into a better home, I raised my children responsibly and I served in my community—and you left me broken and battered because you failed to act on health-care reform. Just as I have come out of the shadows of economic ruin and shame, so too will others come forward to hold you accountable. Remember the hardworking people who elected you. Their bankruptcy shame due to medical crisis really is your shame.[9]

I have heard similar stories from other people in South Dakota and across the country. Donna's testimony was notable for its eloquence, but her story is far from uncommon.

Americans with solid, employer-based insurance may believe they are secure, but in our health-care system everyone is just a pink slip, a divorce, or a major illness away from financial disaster. A 2005 study on the link between medical costs and bankruptcy found that "even brief lapses in insurance coverage may be ruinous and should not be viewed as benign," and that even people with insurance can be forced into bankruptcy by high medical bills, because "many health insurance policies prove to be too skimpy in the face of serious illness." Medical debt affects health, families' economic security, and even their jobs. The same study recounted a story that illustrates this:

> For instance, one debtor underwent lung surgery and suffered a heart attack. Both hospitalizations were covered by his employer-based insurance, but he was unable to return to his physically demanding job. He found new employment but was denied coverage because of his preexisting conditions, which required costly ongoing care. Similarly, a teacher who suffered a heart attack was unable to return to work for many months, and hence her coverage lapsed. A hospital wrote off her $20,000 debt, but she was nonetheless bankrupted by doctors' bills and the cost of medications.[10]

Skyrocketing Costs

THERE ARE MANY factors driving up health-care costs. One problem is that powerful "supply-side" forces exist in our health-care system. Physicians both diagnose and treat illness— in economic terms, they create and satisfy demand. Patients rarely question doctors' decisions, even though some medical procedures have little benefit, once costs are taken into account. Furthermore, the health-care industry has expanded its scope: Conditions such as "restless leg syndrome" weren't conditions until drugs were developed to treat them. As David Mechanic, a health-care policy expert at Rutgers University, noted in his recent book, "more and more of what were once seen as social, behavioral, or normative aspects of everyday life, or as normal processes of aging, are now framed in a medical context. . . . Whether wrinkles, breasts, or buttocks, impotence or social anxieties, or inattention in school, they all have become grist for the medical mill."[11] The proliferation of direct-to-consumer advertising has fueled patient demand for these drugs. Manufacturers of both drugs and medical devices often pay for conferences and shower doctors with gifts as they try to expand the market for their products. In some cases, the integrity of respected medical journals has been compromised. Some studies have suggested that physicians are too quick to employ expensive treatments and procedures on patients who don't stand to benefit from them.

For twenty years, John Abramson was a family physician in a town north of Boston. He considered himself lucky to have found his true calling, but he was so disgusted by these trends that he decided to give up his practice. In his book *Overdosed America*, Abramson recalls how he tried to explain his decision to a longtime patient.

> I explained that tests unlikely to improve patient care were being routinely ordered and expensive drugs that had not been shown to be any more effective or safer than the older drugs they were replacing were being routinely prescribed . . . much of the "scientific evidence" on which doctors must rely to guide our clinical decisions was being commercially spun, or worse; and that many of the articles published in even the most respected medical journals seemed more like infomercials whose purpose was to promote their sponsors' products, rather than to search for the best ways to improve people's health.[12]

But it would be a mistake to lay the blame entirely on health-care providers and drug companies. The use and overuse of new technologies and treatments is grounded in American culture. Americans are imbued with a can-do spirit, and an abiding faith in technological innovation. More so than people in other countries, they just aren't inclined to fatalistically accept a hopeless diagnosis or forgo experimental interventions if there is even the slightest chance of success. In one recent survey, 34 percent of Americans said they believed that modern medicine could cure almost any illness for people who had access to the most advanced technology and treatment. Only 27 percent of Canadians and 11 percent of Germans expressed that view. Two-thirds of Americans say they are "very interested" in news of new medical discoveries, while only 44 percent of Europeans say they are.[13] Richard A. Deyo and Donald L. Patrick explore this idea in their 2005 book on our nation's obsession with medical advances.

> We're a "technoconsumptive" culture. We're pulled irresistibly to new technology, often without recognizing the risks. We seem to assume that high-tech medicine can only be better than low-tech medicine, that more medical care is better, that newer is better, and that more aggressive is better. Yet sometimes it isn't so. In a study of more aggressive care versus more conservative care for certain patients with heart disease, the more aggressive strategy—with more cardiac catheterization and balloon angioplasty—was associated with a higher death rate. The implication was that sometimes the more aggressive strategy is followed without a clear reason.[14]

The consolidation of the health-care industry also is inflating costs. In 2006, a study by the Government Accountability Office found that in most states only a handful of companies sold health insurance policies to small businesses. With little competition, employers and individuals have to pay the high prices set by the dominant insurers and hospitals. Expensive new technologies and procedures are a major factor, too. Nobody wants to deny patients the benefits of these advancements to save money. But because our system is so convoluted, we may be paying more for them than we should. One recent study found that Americans paid more for prescription drugs, hospitals, and doctors' visits than people in comparable nations. The study concluded that it is this price gap that drives U.S. health-care costs, and not that Americans utilize medical care more frequently.[15]

Another factor is that the fragmented and uncoordinated system for insuring people in the United States gives purchasers little power to negotiate for lower prices. As a result, half of the profits in the drug industry worldwide are paid for by Americans.[16] Moreover, we pay—perhaps two to three times as much as countries such as Great Britain—for the complexity, marketing costs, and insurance overhead that result from our market-oriented system.[17] In 2003, a study published in the *New England Journal of Medicine* by three Harvard researchers concluded that 31 percent of every dollar spent on health care in the United States is consumed by administrative costs. In Canada, the percentage is less than 17 percent.[18] Surveys suggest that American doctors and nurses spend between one-third and one-half of their time completing paperwork. As a percentage of overall health spending, our administrative costs are more than three times higher than those of the most efficient nations (France, Finland, and Japan), and between 20 percent and 30 percent higher than the rate in Switzerland and Germany, two other countries where private insurers play a substantial role. If we could match the efficiency of the leading nations, we'd save about $85 billion a year, according to the Commonwealth Fund.[19]

We've all seen stories on the nightly news about desperately sick or injured foreigners who come to the United States seeking high-tech treatments they can't get at home. But the high cost of care in this country is forcing a growing number of Americans to become "medical tourists" themselves. Bumrungrad International Hospital in Bangkok, for example, attracted 65,000 American patients in 2006. One of them, a sixty-one-year-old uninsured Alaskan woman named Sherry Louise Pinkly, told National Public Radio that in Thailand she paid $20,000 for knee replacement surgery that would have cost her more than $100,000 at home. Pinkly's husband, Gordon, said the couple ended up paying a lower price for more attentive care. "The doctors are in here once or twice a day. And there's always nursing staff here taking care of her," Gordon Pinkly told NPR. "(A) Third World hospital, to me, is a hospital in the United States where you lay on a gurney in the emergency room for an hour and a half before you're seen."[20]

Unpaid Bills Become Hidden Taxes

THE PROBLEMS OF coverage and cost are, of course, inextricably linked. As a condition for receiving federal money, most hospital emergency rooms have to provide care to people who desperately need it, whether they are insured or not. But if a patient doesn't have health insurance and can't afford to pay the bill, the bill doesn't just vanish—it is passed on to everybody else. Physicians and hospitals charge higher fees to cover the cost of the free care, and insurers pass on the higher costs to people with insurance by restricting benefits or raising deductibles and premiums.

Sometimes, providers try to recoup the cost of the free care they give to uninsured, low-income people by inflating the bills of middle-class people who are either uninsured or underinsured. The very poor are covered by Medicaid, so middle-class families with some assets are an attractive target. A few years ago, *The Wall Street Journal* featured the story of Paul Shipman, a forty-two-year-old Virginia man who was admitted to the hospital after experiencing chest pains. Suspecting a heart attack, doctors at Inova Fairfax Hospital performed a cardiac catheterization to examine and unblock Shipman's coronary arteries. They also inserted a stent to prop open a blocked artery. At the time, Shipman and his wife had an income of about $80,000, but they didn't have health coverage. Shipman's wife had quit her job to go back to college, and the couple figured that since they were relatively young and healthy, they could get by without insurance. When he awoke from the surgery, Shipman was so worried about the bill that he ignored medical advice and immediately checked out of the hospital. His fears were well-founded: Inova Fairfax charged him $29,000 for his twenty-one-hour stay. On top of that, the cardiologist gave Shipman a bill for $6,800 and he was told he owed $1,000 for the ambulance trip. Shipman was the victim of a bizarre practice in our irrational system: a heavy markup for people without insurance. Virginia Medicaid officials told the *Journal* they would have been charged far less, about $6,000 for Shipman's night in the hospital and as little as $165 for the ambulance ride, if Shipman had been a Medicaid patient. He wasn't. Even private insurers typically pay only 70 percent to 80 percent of what providers charge. Among the marked-up charges: The hospital billed Shipman $2,114 for the two "balloons" used to open up his clogged arteries, even though it paid less than $600 for them. And it charged $7,560 for the stent, even though the manufacturer listed it at an undiscounted price of $3,195.[21]

Another *Journal* article, published in 2003, provoked such outrage it led to calls for greater government oversight of the billing practices of nonprofit hospitals. It told the story of

Quinton White, a seventy-seven-year old man who was struggling to pay $40,000 he owed to Yale–New Haven Hospital for care his wife received when she was suffering from cancer. The kicker: Yale–New Haven treated Jeanette White's cancer in 1983, and she died in 1993. Over the years, White had paid the hospital $16,000, nearly all of the $18,740 he originally owed, but the hospital charged 10 percent interest. The hospital's lawyer got a lien on the Whites' house in 1983, and nearly cleaned out Quinton White's bank account in 1996.[22]

Jeanette White's medical bills were extreme, but the story illustrates a broader point: Every player in our health-care system is intent on shifting costs rather than reducing them.

Economic Drag

THERE IS NO doubt that exploding insurance premiums are sapping the strength of American companies that continue to offer coverage to their workers: In the past ten years, the cost of health care to businesses has increased 140 percent. Since 2000, the cost of premiums for employer-based plans has outpaced wage growth by nearly fivefold.[23] By 2008, there is a real prospect that health costs will exceed the profits of Fortune 500 companies.[24]

I recall a conversation I had not too long ago with the owner of five grocery stores in the Washington, D.C., area. Eight years ago, he said, he paid 100 percent of the insurance premiums for his 117 workers and their families. Then high costs forced him to decrease his contribution to 75 percent. When I last spoke to him, he had dropped his share to 50 percent and eliminated coverage for workers' families. He also admitted that he now seeks out younger, healthier employees, especially those younger than thirty-eight, the age at which insurance rates increase.

The president and CEO of a company in my native South Dakota that manufactures steam cleaners and pressure washers told me that his firm's health-care costs have been increasing at about three times the inflation rate, which is typical. To lower insurance costs, he purchased a plan that forces his forty employees to pay a $500 annual deductible, up from $200. He also requires prospective employees to fill out a four-page form about their health, and new hires with pre-existing conditions have to pay more for their insurance. He spends about $170,000 a year to cover his workers, a whopping 13 percent of his total payroll.

In many states, insurance companies can hit employers with huge premium hikes when even a single worker has a significant health problem. *The New York Times* recently told the story of Varney's Book Store, a family-owned business in Manhattan, Kansas. Several years ago, a Varney's employee in her midseventies died after a long struggle with emphysema. The next year, the bookstore's insurer raised its premiums by 28 percent, even though most of the other three dozen employees were much younger and healthier than their deceased colleague. Year after year, the store's premiums have continued to increase. Large companies have the clout to fight unreasonable premium hikes, or can insure themselves. Either way, they can spread their health costs over a larger group of employees, minimizing the overall impact. But small employers can't take advantage of those economies of scale, and many of them can't afford to insure themselves. No wonder small-business employees are one of the fastest-growing segments of the uninsured, and now comprise about one-fifth of the total. "Almost any kind of situation where one employee has a serious health condition almost makes the group uninsurable, because of the cost." Kansas Governor Kathleen Sebelius told *The New York Times:* "Affordable coverage for small-business owners and self-employed individuals is probably the biggest challenge that we have in Kansas and most states."[25]

A small firm that opts to scale back or eliminate coverage for its workers may be making a rational financial decision—in the short run. In the long run, however, that decision only feeds the relentless rise of health-care costs in society at large by swelling the ranks of the uninsured.

Skeptics say we can't afford to cover everyone; the truth is that we can't afford not to. Our large uninsured population and fast-rising health costs are huge impediments to our economic competitiveness. The Institute of Medicine estimates that our economy loses as much as $130 billion each year because of the untreated illnesses of uninsured Americans. Uninsured workers tend to be absent more than those with insurance, and they are more likely to switch jobs—both of which diminish firms' productivity. Furthermore, the fear of going without health insurance dissuades many people from starting their own businesses, to the detriment of our overall economy.

Many American companies, including our struggling automakers, operate at a distinct disadvantage because of the high cost of health coverage. Ford and GM pay nearly $1,500 in health-care costs for each vehicle they produce, while BMW pays $450 per vehicle in Germany and Honda $150 per vehicle in Japan. Health care has become such a central issue for GM that *The Economist* magazine only partly in jest called the company a "pension hedge fund and health insurance business that happens to make cars." No wonder one GM executive told me that the high cost of health care is the single largest impediment to creating more jobs in the United States. Other major industries are feeling the same pressure. An IBM executive, Senior Vice President for Human Resources J. Randall McDonald, recently predicted that "five years from now this problem will have to be cured, or the competitiveness of the United States will be dramatically affected."[26]

A general distrust of government leads some businesses to believe that they will pay even more under a reformed health-care system. But most other industrialized nations manage to pay for universal health care without levying special taxes on corporations or even mandating that employers provide coverage to their workers. In World Bank rankings of the best places in the world to do business, the United States typically trails countries such as New Zealand and Finland, where all citizens have health coverage.

Crumbling Coverage

OUR SYSTEM RELIES on employers to subsidize health insurance, but the number of Americans with employer-sponsored coverage has steadily declined in the past three decades, from 70 percent in the mid-1970s to 64 percent in 2000 to less than 60 percent in 2006.[27] Rising premiums are one reason, but the drop also is due to the increasing number of independent contractors, temporary employees, and part-time employees in the U.S. workforce. Many companies provide health benefits only to full-time employees. Some of the uninsured are workers who have lost their jobs because of layoffs, or other factors beyond their control. Some of these people can remain temporarily on their employer's plan through the federal COBRA law or a similar state program, but it is expensive to do so: An unemployed worker must pay the employer's full cost of the coverage plus a 2 percent administrative fee. Many believe that Medicaid is the safety net for everyone in desperate financial straits, but each state has different eligibility rules, and in forty-two of them, poor adults without dependents never qualify. A parent in a family of three working full-time at minimum wage would earn too much to qualify for Medicaid in twenty-five states.[28]

There are so many young adults who lack health coverage, the insurance industry has a name for them: "the young invincibles." Many adults in their twenties are too old to be covered by their parents' policies (most insurers drop children from their parents' policies once they turn nineteen or finish school) and Medicaid and SCHIP reclassify them as adults as soon as they turn nineteen. Many young adults in their twenties move in and out of school and jobs, making it difficult to secure a stable and consistent source of health insurance. When they are working, many of them have jobs—as waiters, bike messengers, bartenders, and the like—that don't offer coverage. According to some estimates, almost half of young Americans between the ages of nineteen and twenty-three lack health coverage during all or part of a given year.[29] In 2004, there were 13.7 million uninsured adults between the ages of nineteen and twenty-nine, 2.5 million more than in 2000. The most recent statistics indicate that even though young adults between nineteen and twenty-nine make up about 17 percent of the under-sixty-five U.S. population, they are 30 percent of the nonelderly uninsured. In a 2005 survey, more than one third of young adults, both insured and uninsured, said they had problems paying medical bills or were paying off medical debts over time.[30]

Young adults are the largest and fastest growing group of uninsured. They also are likely to visit the emergency room with an injury, placing themselves and their families at considerable financial risk. The story of Trent MacNamara, a twenty-seven-year-old fact-checker at the magazine *GQ*, illustrates the vulnerability of many young Americans. MacNamara was riding his bike in New York City when the door of the garbage truck in front of him opened suddenly. He slammed into the door and was thrown to the pavement, and while he was lying dazed on the street, the Jeep Cherokee cruising behind him ran over his arm. Miraculously, he wasn't seriously hurt. "Once I realized I was more or less alright, the first thing that went through my head was that I didn't have insurance," MacNamara recalled in a *New York* magazine article. "When the paramedics arrived, I pleaded with them to let me go. I kept asking if they thought I had broken ribs, and they kept saying they weren't qualified. Finally, they told me that if I could breathe without pain, they probably weren't broken. I promised them I would walk to the hospital. I just limped to the subway and went home."[31]

Casualties of the "System"

TRENT MACNAMARA'S HELMET—and luck—saved him from disaster. But the absence of health-care coverage shortens many people's lives: The Institute of Medicine estimates that a lack of health insurance leads to 18,000 unnecessary deaths each year. Some people warn that covering everybody will lead to waiting lists and health-care "rationing." But the United States has its own type of rationing—rationing based on income, insurance status, and illness. In one study, 57 percent of lower-income adults said they went without needed medical care, did not get recommended tests or follow-up care, or skipped taking their prescriptions to save money.[32] Many people who are uninsured or underinsured forgo cancer screenings and other preventive care, delay treatment for their medical conditions, or skimp on drugs. When a serious illness is permitted to progress, a patient is less likely to survive and care is more expensive. A recent study published in the *Journal of the American Medical Association* found that people who had trouble paying their medical bills did significantly worse after heart attacks than patients who weren't under financial pressure. Although most of the 2,500 patients in the study had insurance, almost 20 percent of them said they had avoided health care in the previous year because they couldn't afford it. The researchers found that there were 12 percent more cases of angina among the financially troubled patients, and they were readmitted to the hospital at a rate 11 percent higher than other patients. Patients who skipped medications for financial reasons were 50 percent more likely to be readmitted.[33]

Studies have shown that starts and stops in coverage can damage a person's health as much as being continuously uninsured, and in our employer-based system, many people cycle on and off insurance when they switch jobs or leave the workforce. In 2004 and 2005, nearly 82 million Americans were without insurance for at least part of those two years.[34] This is a particular problem for women, who are more likely than men to work part-time or leave the workforce for some period of time to care for children.

The story of Dee Dee Dodd, thirty-eight, puts a human face on the problem. Dodd, who lives with her husband and four children near Austin, Texas, has insulin-dependent diabetes but can't afford health insurance. For many years, she visited the doctor only occasionally and tried to self-manage her condition to save money. The results were disastrous. During one eighteen-month period, Dodd was rushed almost monthly to the emergency room with episodes of ketoacidosis, a chemical imbalance that sometimes put her into life-threatening comas. By neglecting her condition for so long, Dodd had weakened her body and developed preventable side effects like esophageal ulcers. She ended up spending weeks in intensive care and racked up $191,000 in unpaid bills. "I had to stop working, so then I couldn't afford to go to the doctor, and then I had to go to the emergency room," the former dental assistant told *The New York Times*. Eventually, the Seton Family of Hospitals in the Austin area began offering Dodd free primary care, figuring that regular medical attention would be less expensive than Dodd's emergency-room visits. Seton paid for a $3,200 insulin pump, an endocrinologist, and home counseling for Dodd. Her health improved, and in eighteen months the hospital saved $86,580.[35]

How do people with chronic health problems get by without going to the doctor? Consider the story of John, a fifty-one-year-old Idaho man who manages a bar that doesn't offer him health coverage. John, who wouldn't reveal his last name, shared his story with two researchers who traveled the country interviewing people without insurance. He told them he had been injured numerous times over the years—including being pinned under a rig for four hours when he was a young man, being hit in the head with a combine, and several falls from ladders—but these injuries mostly went untreated because he couldn't afford proper medical care. As a result, he now has chronic pain in his back, ribs, and legs, and needs medication just to get out of bed in the morning. On a typical day, he told them, he takes eight ibuprofen pills every two hours, even though the maximum recommended dosage is six pills in a twenty-four-hour period. John has painful bone spurs on both feet, but because surgery would cost more than $1,000, it is out of the question. Instead, he takes matters into his own hands:

> I just take a tool, and I shave it. I have to do that like twice a week, get it down to where I can walk on it. I just take that spur and put the sander to it. Squint your eyes and grit your teeth. It really hurts, especially when it hits the real skin. I can shave it down, and three days later it's right back to where it started. . . . It's hard to live without health insurance, I'm here to tell you. I mean, there are times when I should've gone to the doctor, but I couldn't afford to go because I don't have insurance. Like when my back messed up, I should've gone. If I had insurance, I would've went, because I know I could get treatment; but when you can't afford it, you don't go. Because the harder the hole you get into in terms of bills, then you'll never get out. So you just say, "I can deal with the pain."[36]

High deductibles are another barrier to consistent care. Eleven million people with health insurance have per-person deductibles of $1,000 or more. One recent study found that 44 percent of adults with deductibles of $1,000 or more didn't fill a prescription, declined to see a specialist, skipped a recommended test or treatment, or didn't see a doctor when they had a serious medical problem. About 22 percent of adults with deductibles under $500 reported the same behavior. Forty-one percent of people with deductibles of $1,000 or more said they owed money for medical bills.[37]

Being sick also makes it harder to get coverage in the first place. American insurance companies employ underwriting strategies that exclude or charge the highest rates to people who need the coverage the most. People with "pre-existing conditions" such as high blood pressure often have to pay higher premiums than healthy people, and those with more serious medical conditions may not be able to get coverage at all. In one recent survey, nine in ten people who tried to obtain individual coverage on the private market never bought a plan, either because they couldn't afford it or because they were turned down. More than half of those who did buy coverage said it cost them at least $3,000 a year.[38] In 2007, the average cost of family coverage was $12,106.[39]

Federal Policy Failures

THE FEDERAL GOVERNMENT'S patchwork of health-care programs is just as irrational as the private "system." A diabetic veteran might have full prescription coverage, while a diabetic senior who didn't serve in the military might have none. A low-income woman with breast cancer might be covered by Medicaid, while a woman with lung cancer might not. The child of a marine might have better benefits than the child of a National Guardsman, despite equal service and sacrifice by their parents. Incredibly, until just recently members of the National Guard and reserves did not get any health-care coverage from the Pentagon. This despite the fact that since September 11, 2001, we have seen dramatic increases in the frequency and duration of overseas deployments for guard and reserves—deployments that often lead to a loss of employer-based coverage. Working with a Republican colleague of mine, Senator Lindsey Graham of South Carolina, I was able to boost coverage for National Guardsmen and reserves in 2002, 2003, and 2004. Remarkably, the most vigorous opposition to our efforts came from Secretary of Defense Donald Rumsfeld, who balked at the cost of expanding coverage.

Congress's dismal performance in providing sensible health benefits to its beneficiaries is probably inevitable. Local hospitals, doctors, health-care suppliers, and others all have homes—and members of Congress—in different parts of the country. Reducing Medicare coverage for any service or treatment is the equivalent of closing a military base in its economic impact in some cases. Moreover, health-care suppliers typically ally themselves with patient advocates, who view Medicare policy changes as matters of life and death. Some of the most potent advocacy comes from lawmakers themselves, since many of them have had their own experiences with painful or deadly diseases, either personally or through relatives and friends. The result is a set of coverage policies across Medicare, Medicaid, and the Veterans Administration that is utterly incoherent.

Consider the catch-22 that vexes million of people with disabilities. When Medicare was expanded to cover certain people with disabilities in 1972, the federal government established a two-year waiting period. The idea was to keep costs down by making sure that only those with long-term problems would qualify. The rule exempts those suffering from end-stage kidney disease or, more recently, Lou Gehrig's disease. But it denies much-needed help to many others who are too ill to work, too ill to get private insurance, and receive too much in Social Security disability payments to qualify for Medicaid. Roxianna McCutchan, a clerk and dispatcher at the police department in Rockford, Texas, was trapped in this unenviable situation.

McCutchan, thirty-six, had to quit her job in 2002 when a rare muscle disorder twisted her spine and compressed her lungs, making it difficult for her to breathe. McCutchan qualified for $796 a month from Social Security, but that wasn't enough to pay her share of the insurance she had through her old job, and no private insurance company would cover her, because of the seriousness of her condition. The $796 a month was too much, however, for her to qualify for Medicaid. Even with free medical care from her doctor and oxygen donated by her church, McCutchan ended up in the hospital four times in 2003. By the time she finally qualified for Medicare in 2005, she weighed seventy-three pounds and was $20,000 in debt. "Asking for help and relying on the kindness of a doctor takes away your pride and dignity, your self-esteem," McCutchan told *USA Today*.[40]

Global Myths About U.S. Health Care

OUR SYSTEM IS so disjointed it's no wonder we measure up so poorly to other nations when it comes to prevention and care management. Australia has vaccinated more seniors against flu and children against polio.[41] The United States has a higher incidence of Hepatitis B, a vaccine-preventable disease, than do Australia, Canada, and New Zealand, and a higher asthma mortality rate than Australia or Canada.[42]

Defenders of the current system insist that Americans with insurance get the best health care in the world. But can we say we have the best system when our infant mortality rate is twenty-eighth in the world—and rising in some areas? Can we say we have the best system when only 30 percent of sick Americans can get same-day care, while in the United Kingdom the percentage is 45 percent? Overall, American adults receive recommended care only about half the time, according to one study.[43] The Canadian health-care system, much-maligned during the American health-care debate of the early 1990s, gives patients better odds of surviving colorectal cancer and childhood leukemia than the U.S. system.[44] Our survival rates are lower than Australians for cervical cancer and non-Hodgkin's lymphoma, and the likelihood of surviving a kidney transplant is 13 percent higher in Canada, 6 percent higher in Australia, and 4 percent higher in the United Kingdom and New Zealand.[45]

These outcomes reflect sporadic quality of care. More than 30 percent of adults in the United States—a higher percentage than in comparable countries—have problems with coordination of care, meaning test results or medical records were not available at the time of a scheduled appointment; patients received duplicate tests or procedures; patients received conflicting information; or some combination of these problems.[46] Furthermore, 15 percent of American patients reported being given incorrect test results or experiencing delays in being told about abnormal results, again a higher percentage than in comparable nations.[47] In an influential 2000 study, the Institute of Medicine estimated that as many as 98,000 Americans die annually from medical errors, caused by bad physician handwriting, incomplete charts, or other "low-tech" problems. Preventable errors also exact a heavy financial toll, costing as much as $29 billion annually, according to the institute. Its report cites "the decentralized and fragmented nature of the health delivery system" as the cause of many of the mistakes.[48]

Even within hospitals and large medical groups, there are rigidly defined areas of specialization and influence. For example, when patients see multiple providers in different settings, none of whom have access to complete information, it is easier for something to go wrong than when care is better coordinated. At the same time, the provision of care to patients by a collection of loosely affiliated organizations and providers makes it difficult to implement improved clinical information systems capable of providing timely access to complete patient information. Unsafe care is one of the prices we pay for not having organized systems of care with clear lines of accountability.[49]

One disturbing characteristic of our health system that also distinguishes us from peer nations is that members of racial and ethnic minorities tend to get worse care than whites. In large part, this is because minorities are far more likely to be uninsured. According to a 2005 survey, nearly two thirds of working-age Hispanics and one third of African Americans were without coverage for at least part of that year, compared with 20 percent of working-age whites. Hispanics in particular were disconnected from the health-care system: Only 37 percent of uninsured Hispanics said they had a regular doctor, compared with 66 percent of African Americans and 62 percent of whites. Having a regular place to go for care leads to better treatment of chronic conditions and increases the likelihood that an illness will be detected at an early stage.[50]

The infant mortality rate for African-American babies is 2.5 times higher than it is for whites, and the rate for Native Americans is 1.5 times higher.[51] Overall, mortality was 31 percent higher for blacks than for whites in 2004.[52] Nationwide, life expectancy for African Americans is five years shorter than it is for whites, but the gap is even greater in poorer areas.

Black women are more than twice as likely to die from cervical cancer as white women and are more likely to die of breast cancer than women in any other group.[53] Lower rates of coverage are responsible for some of these disparities, but different treatment, even when insured, also is a factor. A recent study found that among Medicare beneficiaries, white patients were more likely to receive high-cost procedures than black patients.[54] In spite of their higher mortality and morbidity for heart disease, blacks and Hispanics are less likely to receive treatment and are especially less likely to get high-tech cardiac procedures such as cardiac catheterization and coronary revascularization.[55]

Although we've made dramatic progress in reducing the stigma attached to mental illness, our system still gives short shrift to mental health. Some programs set limits on mental health care that don't exist for treatment of physical ailments. Many private insurers set higher deductibles and co-payments for mental health benefits, or place limits on the number of times patients can receive outpatient or inpatient care. In 2002, a presidential panel concluded that our mental health system is "fragmented, disconnected, and often inadequate."[56]

We take great pride in our high-tech medical equipment, but our health-care system is incredibly primitive when it comes to using the information systems that are common in American workplaces. Only 15 to 20 percent of clinicians have computerized patient records, and only a small fraction of the billions of medical transactions that take place each year in the United States are conducted electronically. Studies suggest that this weakness compromises the quality of care, leads to medical errors, and costs us as much as $78 billion a year.[57] A landmark report issued by the Institute of Medicine in 2001 noted that "health-care delivery has been relatively untouched by the revolution in information technology that has been transforming nearly every other aspect of society." Little has changed since then.

> The meticulous collection of personal health information throughout a patient's life can be one of the most important inputs to the provision of proper care. Yet for most individuals, that health information is dispersed in a collection of paper records that are poorly organized and often illegible, and frequently cannot be retrieved in a timely fashion, making it nearly impossible to manage many forms of chronic illness that require frequent monitoring and ongoing patient support.[58]

We are years, if not decades, behind European nations in harnassing in health-care information technology's potential.

Long-term care is another troubling area—and the only one in which we spend less compared to peer nations. As the baby boomers age, paying for long-term care will become a pressing problem for more Americans. The over-sixty-five population will grow from 36 million in 2000 to 78 million in 2040, according to the U.S. Census Bureau. The prevalence of disability among the elderly has been steadily decreasing, but life expectancy is getting longer. Long-term care coverage under Medicare is limited, since it has to be connected to a hospital discharge. Medicaid pays for long-term care, but it is targeted to the poorest people, and many who have too much money to qualify simply cannot afford paid help. Furthermore, the program is still fundamentally geared toward institutional care, even though most elderly people prefer to receive care at home or in more personalized community settings. Long-term care insurance is available on the private market, but few employers offer it at a group discount, and studies have indicated that less than 20 percent of the elderly can afford to purchase it on their own.[59] David Mechanic calls long-term care "the stepchild of our health-care system." According to Mechanic, long-term care vividly exhibits our system's inability to deal with chronic conditions in an integrated way.

> Long-term care services in the United States are expensive, difficult to organize and coordinate, insufficiently comprehensive, and do not do a good enough job of meeting the needs of elders, families and other informal caregivers. To make a bad situation worse, the care is of uneven quality across settings, whether in nursing homes, assisted-care facilities, foster care homes, patients' own homes, or elsewhere in the community. Doctors and nurses try hard despite poorly organized care arrangements to take good care of persons with chronic diseases and disabilities, but they are thwarted by the difficulty of implementing well-designed disease-management approaches and by limited opportunities for effective use of multidisciplinary approaches and teams.[60]

To be sure, there are elements of our health system that are excellent. The United States has the best rates of Pap tests and mammograms for women, and the odds of surviving breast cancer are 14 percent higher here than in the United Kingdom. We have some of the world's best specialists, and a training system that attracts people from all over the world. We are recognized as world leaders in technological innovation and ground-breaking research, and people with good coverage can choose from a wide range of providers. But considering what we spend on health care in this country, we should be able to provide care that is far and away the best on the planet. Health care is a complex topic, but we have to face a simple truth: We're paying top dollar for mediocre results.

Signs of Change

FRUSTRATED BY INACTION at the federal level, many
states are acting on their own to expand coverage and curb
costs. In Massachusetts in 2006, former Republican Governor
Mitt Romney worked with a Democrat-dominated legislature
to craft a plan that will cover all but about 65,000 of the state's
328,000 uninsured adults. Massachusetts has a population of
about 6 million people, so when the plan is fully implemented about 99 percent of the state's residents will have
coverage. Vermont also approved a law in 2006 designed to
cover all or nearly all of its residents. California Governor
Arnold Schwarzenegger, another Republican governor in an
overwhelmingly Democratic state, has proposed his own universal coverage plan. Many states want to raise the income
limits for the State Children's Health Insurance Program, a
joint state-federal program, while others have taken action to
cover young adults and cut the cost of health insurance for
small employers.

Most striking, however, is that doctors, hospitals, insurers, and large employers—strident opponents of previous health reform efforts—are now calling for change. In January 2007, sixteen groups, including the U.S. Chamber of Commerce, the American Hospital Association, the American Medical Association, the Blue Cross and Blue Shield Association, Pfizer, Johnson & Johnson, Kaiser Permanente, AARP, and America's Health Insurance Plans (a trade group for insurers) called for more money for the State Children's Health Insurance Program and new tax credits for individuals and families struggling to afford private insurance.[61] The next month, AT&T, Wal-Mart, Intel, and Kelly Services, the temporary-staffing company, joined with the Communication Workers of America, the Service Employees International Union, and think tanks such as the Center for American Progress to call for a new American health-care system by 2012. "The system is going to break. You can only put so many uninsured people through the emergency rooms before employers stop offering coverage," warned Carl T. Camden, president and chief executive of Kelly Services.[62] Each member of the coalition signed a "principles document" beginning with the following passage:

> America's health care system is broken. The traditional employer-based model of coverage in its current form is endangered without substantial reform to our health care system. It is being crushed by out of control costs, the pressures of the global economy, and the large and growing number of the uninsured. Soaring health costs threaten workers' livelihoods and companies' competitiveness, and

undermine the security that individuals of a prosperous nation should enjoy. We can only solve these problems— and deliver health care that is high quality, affordable, accessible, and secure—if business, government, labor, the health care delivery system and the nonprofit sector work together.

Ensuring that all Americans have access to affordable, efficient, high-quality health care is absolutely essential to our country's well-being. As Thomas Jefferson put it, "Without health, there is no happiness." Indisputably, the American public is dissatisfied with the current health-care system and eager for change. A *New York Times*/CBS News poll conducted in February 2007 found that a majority of Americans wanted the federal government to guarantee health insurance to every citizen. Sixty percent of respondents, including 62 percent of independents and 46 percent of Republicans, said they'd be willing to pay more in taxes to ensure that every American is covered. Half said they'd be willing to pay as much as $500 a year. An overwhelming majority said the U.S. health-care system needs fundamental change or total reorganization.[63]

But there were similar poll results in the early 1990s, when President Clinton launched the last major attempt at health-care reform. And at that time too, prominent business leaders expressed support for the idea of universal coverage, even a "play-or-pay" proposal that would have forced them to either insure their workers or pay into a fund for the uninsured. How can we make sure that today's fledgling health-care effort doesn't fall victim to the forces that doomed the previous ones? We need to get beyond the partisan paralysis that says we can't find a health-care system that works for both business and workers. I simply don't believe that. We can find a solution, and the Federal Health Board I am proposing, or something similar, should be part of it.

Part Two

THE HISTORY OF HEALTH REFORM

The tortuous history of health reform in the last century illuminates our current predicament, offering lessons we shouldn't ignore if we want to finally fix our broken system. As a member of the Senate leadership in the early 1990s, I was an active participant in our country's last major health-care debate. But my intense interest in the issue predated President Clinton's attempt to reform the system, and it continued after his effort unraveled. My colleagues and I made some progress on health care during my twenty-six years on Capitol Hill, but the successes were incremental ones, and frankly they were outweighed by the failures. By the time I left Congress in 2005, I had come to believe that no other issue was as complex, as personal, and as fiercely contested by special interests as health care. The characters and the details have changed through the decades, but the pattern of failure on health-care reform has remained remarkably constant.

Early Efforts

UNTIL THE BEGINNING of the twentieth century, medical care in the United States was inexpensive because it was largely ineffective. The steady march of medical progress began in the 1910s, when doctors learned how to prevent infection and refined the use of anesthesia. But medicine began to cost more as it became more advanced, and neither the government nor private companies offered health insurance. Those who couldn't afford to pay out-of-pocket either went without treatment or ran up huge debts.[1] When Progressive Era reformers turned their attention to workers' health, they decided to put compulsory health insurance on the national agenda for the first time. In 1914, the American Association for Labor Legislation began drafting legislation to provide workers with free medical care, paid sick leave, and a modest death benefit. By 1917, the AALL bill had been introduced in fourteen state legislatures.[2] The fate of the legislation foreshadowed the health insurance debates that occurred throughout the twentieth century.

Only California and New York seriously considered the measure, and the battle in California didn't last long. Physicians, fearing that any third-party payer, especially the government, would regulate doctors' fees, vigorously opposed it. They were allied with the insurance companies, which worried that government health insurance would undermine the private life insurance market. In a 1918 referendum, the measure was soundly defeated.[3] In New York the legislation faced opposition from the same quarters. Doctors from New York City were supportive, but those from upstate and rural areas said the proposal smacked of socialism, a loaded charge in the midst of the Red scare. When the New York Senate approved the bill, employers and insurance companies were spurred to action. The employers created a special committee to discredit AALL estimates of workers' illnesses, and began examining the feasibility of employer-sponsored insurance as an alternative. Some unions supported the bill, but others joined with employers to fight it. Samuel Gompers, president of the American Federation of Labor (AFL), denounced the proposal as "a menace to the rights, welfare, and liberty of American workers." The New York bill died in committee in 1919, but it wasn't long before some insurance companies acted to blunt the appeal of government-sponsored health insurance by offering their own coverage.[4] According to historian Beatrix Hoffman, this episode "contributed to the making of a limited welfare state, a distinctive health-care system, and a political culture and configuration of interest-group power that would resist universal health coverage for the rest of the century."[5] Indeed, even after the Soviet Union and the Cold War receded into history, opponents of national health insurance would raise the specter of "socialized medicine" to great effect.

The Depression sparked the creation of more private insurance plans and another attempt at national health insurance. Because people had so little money, hospital occupancy rates plummeted. In search of a steady source of revenue, hospitals began offering "prepayment" plans to certain groups, such as hospital employees, teachers, and firefighters. For a monthly fee, members were guaranteed free hospital care if they ever needed it.[6] Meanwhile, in 1934 President Franklin Roosevelt launched the Committee on Economic Security to craft the Social Security Act. After the advisory panel included national health insurance in a preliminary report, doctors mobilized to stop it. They bombarded Congress with postcards, letters, and phone calls; the president's personal physician even lobbied Eleanor Roosevelt. Worried that national health insurance would sink the entire proposal, which included unemployment insurance and aid to the elderly, widows, single mothers, and poor children, President Roosevelt decided to leave health care out of the final bill.[7]

The hospital prepayment plans endured, evolving into the Blue Cross system and becoming the model for group health insurance as we know it today. One crucial feature of the plans was that they were employment-based—that is, they were offered to groups of workers large enough to spread out the cost of caring for the sick or injured. Still spooked by the prospect of government-sponsored health insurance, many employers accepted the Blue Cross system as a more palatable alternative.[8]

Our employment-based system solidified during World War II, when the federal government exempted "fringe benefits" such as health insurance from wage and price controls. To attract workers, who were scarce because so many men were in the military, some employers offered them generous health coverage. The government's decision to exempt health benefits from personal income taxes accelerated the trend.[9] Unions bolstered the nascent insurance system by cutting their own deals with hospitals and later with the Blue Cross.[10]

Truman

=====

STILL, MILLIONS OF people had no insurance, and when the war ended President Truman was determined to do something about it. As a county judge, he had seen "people turned away from hospitals to die because they had no money for treatment," and he never forgot it.[11] In his November 1945 address to Congress, President Truman noted that in the previous four years nearly 5 million American men had been classified as unfit for military service because of poor health, and that 3 million more had been treated or discharged for physical or mental problems that existed before their induction. "In the past, the benefits of modern medical science have not been enjoyed by our citizens with any degree of equality. Nor are they today. Nor will they be in the future—unless government is bold enough to do something about it," he told the Congress. "We should resolve now that the health of this Nation is a national concern; that financial barriers in the way of attaining health shall be removed; that the health of all its citizens deserves the help of all the Nation." National insurance bills were immediately introduced in both the House and the Senate.

Once again, doctors issued a call to arms. "[If this] Old World scourge is allowed to spread to our New World, [it will] jeopardize the health of our people and gravely endanger our freedom," the *Journal of the American Medical Association* opined.[12] With the doctors' help, Republicans portrayed President Truman's proposal as the latest manifestation of a welfare state that was creeping toward communism. The national insurance bills didn't advance in 1946, and when the GOP seized control of Congress in November of that year, the idea appeared dead. But President Truman's dramatic victory in 1948, which swept the Democrats back into power on Capitol Hill, revived it. Three months after his inauguration, the president's allies introduced a new national health insurance bill. Yet again, the AMA spearheaded opposition, urging doctors to lobby their state and federal lawmakers, contact local newspapers, and place posters and the AMA pamphlet "The Voluntary Way is the American Way" in their waiting rooms. The AMA also recruited insurers and employers as allies, and directed doctors to advise their patients to purchase private, voluntary insurance.[13]

The U.S. Chamber of Commerce produced a pamphlet of its own, "You and Socialized Medicine," which alleged that federal officials wanted to take "another step toward further state socialism and the totalitarian welfare state prevailing in foreign lands."[14] Like the doctors, the Chamber viewed voluntary insurance as a way to head off government intervention, and it urged employers to purchase group insurance plans for their workers. Southern politicians also helped thwart national insurance, because they feared that federal involvement in health care would lead to federal action against segregation. Most hospitals in the South had "white" and "colored" floors, labeled equipment by race, and refused to give staff privileges to black doctors. Until the mid-1960s, Southerners who headed key congressional committees blocked federal health programs or made sure that local officials could control them.[15]

Opponents' efforts steadily eroded support for President Truman's plan. In 1945, 75 percent of Americans said they supported national health insurance, but by 1949 only 21 percent did.[16] By the end of 1949, the Soviet Union had set up a communist government in its section of occupied Germany, and the communists had seized control of mainland China. The communist threat loomed larger than ever, and Americans were particularly susceptible to the suggestion that national health insurance was communist-inspired. Democrats retained control of Congress in the 1950 elections, but Republicans made significant gains; President Truman's drive for national health insurance was stopped in its tracks. "I cautioned Congress against being frightened away from health insurance by the scare words 'socialized medicine,' which some people were bandying about. I wanted no part of socialized medicine, and I knew the American people did not," the former president recalled in his memoirs. "I have had some stormy times as President and have engaged in some vigorous controversies. Democracy thrives on debate and political differences. But I had no patience with the reactionary selfish people and politicians who fought year after year every proposal we made to improve the people's health."[17]

As advocates of national health insurance waged their unsuccessful battle in Washington, unions and employers were busy cementing the private, employer-based system we have today. Business leaders recognized that offering health benefits, disability benefits, and pensions to their workers was the best way to deflate the idea of government intervention. After World War II, the National Association of Manufacturers urged business leaders to actively participate in "the competition for leadership in a welfare economy."[18] In 1950, for the first time, General Motors offered to pay for health insurance and pensions for all its workers. G.M. President Charles E. Wilson viewed national health insurance as a threat to the free market and the autonomy of business owners, and he hoped companies could sidestep it by providing insurance themselves. But Walter Reuther, the national president of the United Auto Workers, believed that everybody, not just G.M. employees, deserved health coverage. Reuther backed President Truman's national health insurance plan, convinced that the best way to create a strong health insurance system was to spread the costs and benefits over the largest possible group.[19] Nevertheless, Reuther accepted the automaker's offer, partly because he believed the proliferation of "fringe benefits" would lead to government-sponsored insurance. Eventually, he said, large industrial employers would have to ask the government to assume the costs—a prediction that appears to be finally coming true.[20]

In the early postwar period, unions were able to extract fringe benefits from G.M. and other industrial giants because those companies faced little competition at home or abroad, and they were making huge profits. American firms such as U.S. Steel, Alcoa, and DuPont were just as dominant in their industries as G.M. was in auto manufacturing. AT&T, a regulated monopoly with guaranteed profits, just padded telephone bills to pay for its workers' health benefits. In industries with a number of smaller players, such as housing construction and women's clothing, the unions used their strength to organize industry-wide health insurance plans. Between 1946 and 1957, the number of workers who had health-care coverage secured through collective bargaining increased from 1 million to 12 million. An additional 20 million of their dependents also were covered.[21] By the mid-1950s, 45 percent of all Americans had hospital insurance, a percentage that rose to 77 percent by 1963.[22]

Despite the downfall of President Truman's plan, Reuther held out hope that the benefits workers won through collective bargaining would smooth the way for an expansion of the welfare state sometime in the future. But large employers viewed collective bargaining as a substitute for an expanded welfare state, not as the precursor to one. Meanwhile, rank and file members of powerful unions lost their enthusiasm for national health insurance as they secured better and better benefits for themselves in each round of collective bargaining.[23] "We certainly don't look to the political structure for our wages and working conditions. We get them our way," said George Meany, secretary-treasurer of the AFL in the late 1940s, foreshadowing this perspective.[24]

These developments contrasted with what happened in Europe. There, organized labor worked through the political system to secure health insurance for every citizen, not just union members. In subsequent decades, broad constituencies backed attempts to expand benefits in European countries, while in America such efforts were bogged down in partisan bickering over who should be covered and how to pay for it.[25]

Another key development in the late 1940s and early 1950s helped create the flawed system we are saddled with today. In the years immediately after the war, the primary insurance providers were Blue Cross and Blue Shield, which were non-profits. Blue Cross and Blue Shield plans were "community-rated," meaning that every member paid the same premiums and received the same benefits. The idea behind this "social insurance" model is that the healthy subsidize the sick. In other words, young people with no health problems agree to pay premiums that probably exceed the value of the health care they will receive, in exchange for the security of knowing that the coverage will be there for them as they get older and less healthy, or if they are confronted with a catastrophic illness or injury. Within a few years, however, for-profit companies entered the health insurance market. They offered lower prices to younger, healthier people by basing premiums on actuarial risk. Community rating could not survive when the youngest and healthiest people—that is, those who used medical services the least—were lured away by the promise of lower premiums. Before long, commercial insurers were utilizing "experience rating," or basing a group's annual premium on its use of services the previous year. Larger firms soon realized that it was less expensive for them to self-insure, or cut their own deals with insurance companies, rather than throwing in their lot with broader groups. Today, most insured workers are in firms that go it alone.[26]

As commercial insurers cherry-picked the young and healthy and community rating diminished, older and sicker Americans found it increasingly difficult to find insurance policies they could afford. This was especially true for the elderly, whose low income and loss of connection with the workplace left them largely uninsured. The unions had a vested interest in government help for the elderly. In the late 1950s and early 1960s, they began to win health benefits for retirees, but these victories came at a high price. With the advent of experience rating, retirees were a significant drain on employers' finances, soaking up money they otherwise might have spent on wage increases. If the government took responsibility for insuring retirees, the unions would be able to bargain for higher wages and better benefits for current workers.[27] The AFL-CIO drafted a bill that would establish a government health care program for the elderly and spearheaded the effort to pass it. Union officials wrote speeches for supportive lawmakers, prepped them for hearings, and provided technical support. The AFL-CIO also created a new group, the National Council of Senior Citizens, to lobby for the measure.[28] To counter the AFL-CIO, 260 commercial insurers banded together in 1958 to form the Health Insurance Association of America. Some individual insurers also began offering policies geared toward the elderly.[29]

Medicare and Medicaid

THE CONFLUENCE OF deepening problems and increasing mobilization paved the way for political action. Reacting to rising pressure, in 1960, Congress passed the Kerr-Mills Act, which gave states federal grants to pay for health care for the elderly poor. But the law didn't quiet calls for a broader approach. In 1963, a Senate committee found that the policy was largely ineffective. Only twenty-eight states had implemented it, and many of them hadn't set aside enough state money to pay for it. Some doctors and hospitals refused to participate because payments were below the prevailing rate, and strict means tests and "family responsibility" rules in some states deterred people from applying.[30]

Public support for a broader plan to help the elderly—now called "Medicare"—was building. By 1962, polls indicated that 69 percent of Americans favored such a measure, and President John F. Kennedy made passing it a legislative priority.[31] President Kennedy was one of the first politicians to appreciate the power of the senior vote, and he had endorsed Medicare during his campaign for the White House in 1960. When the Medicare bill stalled in the House, the president's allies attached it to a welfare bill on the Senate floor. Senators rejected it, but the close 52–48 vote gave supporters hope. President Kennedy introduced the bill again the next year, but this time the House Ways and Means Committee narrowly defeated it 13–12.[32] The AMA reprised the role it had played during President Truman's term. The group ran newspaper, radio, and TV ads decrying Medicare as socialized medicine, and it gave doctors speeches, pamphlets, radio tapes, and scripts to help them sow doubts about the proposal. The AMA also created a political action committee, AMPAC, which recruited the personal doctors of members of Congress to lobby against Medicare. The AMA released research showing that most elderly people could afford to pay for their own medical care, and argued that it was unfair to force workers to support seniors who were wealthy or already insured.[33] But the AMA was hurt by the defection of the American Hospital Association and some commercial insurers, who had become resigned to the need for a government program for the elderly. Hospitals often couldn't collect payment from elderly patients, and some insurers had concluded that covering seniors was unprofitable.[34]

The AMA was able to stall Medicare in Congress, but public support didn't dissipate. When Lyndon Johnson assumed the presidency after President Kennedy was assassinated in November 1963, he believed he had a duty to complete the fallen president's domestic agenda, and he included Medicare in his vision of the Great Society. President Johnson viewed his landslide victory in 1964 as an endorsement of this course, and he was buoyed by huge Democratic majorities in both the House and Senate. In his State of the Union address in 1965, he declared that passing Medicare was one of his top priorities, and Medicare bills were introduced in the House and Senate the same day. Historian Doris Kearns Goodwin has highlighted a confluence of forces that brightened the prospects for Medicare and the other social programs in 1965.

> The shock of Kennedy's death, the civil rights movement, an emerging awareness of the extent and existence of poverty, a reduction of threatening tensions between the United States and the Soviet Union, all helped Americans to focus public energies and perceptions on the problems of their own country. More important was the deepening confidence that sustained economic growth, steadily increasing affluence seemed now an enduring and irreversible reality of American life. Therefore the problem was no longer simply the creation of wealth—that would continue—but how best to apply our riches to the improvement of American life.[35]

When the House Ways and Means Committee began its work that year, the Medicare bill drafted by the AFL-CIO and the Johnson administration was only one of three plans on the table. The AMA was pushing "Eldercare," a slightly expanded version of Kerr-Mills that would help states pay the health insurance costs of the elderly poor. Lobbyists for the insurance company Aetna had their own bill, "Bettercare," which called for a federal subsidy for the purchase of private health insurance. To the surprise of the administration and the unions,

Ways and Means Chairman Wilbur Mills, a conservative Democrat from Arkansas, combined all three proposals into a single bill, his "three-layer cake." Medicare Part A, the first layer, would pay for hospital care, skilled nursing for a limited time, and some home health care. Part B, which was optional, would cover the cost of doctors' visits. And Medicaid, a separate program, was created to help states finance not just long-term care for poor seniors but health-care coverage for other vulnerable Americans like single-parent families and people with disabilities. The combined Medicare proposal fell short of what the administration and the unions had wanted. The elderly would have to pay premiums for Part B coverage and co-payments for many services. Furthermore, prescription drugs, eyeglasses, and long-term care weren't covered; private insurance companies would fill those gaps.[36] Still, the final Medicare bill represented the largest expansion of health-care coverage in American history.

President Johnson was scheduled to sign the Medicare bill in Washington, but at the last minute he came up with another idea: He wanted to hold the ceremony in Independence, Missouri, so former President Truman could attend. Some of President Johnson's aides tried to change his mind, wary of the logistical challenge and of dredging up memories of President Truman's more far-reaching plan for national health insurance. The AMA might even boycott the event, they warned.[37] But LBJ insisted, and he signed the bill on July 30, 1965, in the auditorium of the Harry S. Truman Library in Independence. "I am so proud that this has come to pass in the Johnson administration. But it was really Harry Truman of Missouri who planted the seeds of compassion and duty which have today flowered into care for the sick, and serenity for the fearful,"[38] President Johnson said at the event. He continued:

> No longer will older Americans be denied the healing miracle of modern medicine. No longer will illness crush and destroy the savings that they have so carefully put away over a lifetime so that they might enjoy dignity in their later years. No longer will young families see their own incomes, and their own hopes, eaten away simply because they are carrying out their deep moral obligations to their parents, and to their uncles, and their aunts.[39]

As it turned out, doctors, hospitals, and insurance companies shouldn't have been afraid of Medicare—government-sponsored health insurance for the elderly turned into a financial windfall for all of them. Under Medicare Part A, hospitals were supposed to be fully reimbursed for their costs and physicians were entitled to their "usual and customary fees." But two months before Medicare began operating, the AHA and the Blue Cross convinced federal officials to adopt a reimbursement formula giving the hospitals money for all "allowable" expenses plus a 2 percent bonus above their actual costs with no upper limit. Because the federal government had pledged not to intrude on the sacred doctor-patient relationship, it simply paid the bills without investigating whether providers were charging it too much. Instead, groups of hospitals and nursing homes were empowered to select their own "fiscal intermediaries" to make that determination. About 80 percent of the intermediaries they picked were Blue Cross organizations, which were closely tied to the hospitals. The federal government had to cover the intermediaries' administrative costs.[40]

After Medicare began paying for a limited amount of nursing home care, for-profit nursing homes successfully lobbied Congress for a revised reimbursement formula that paid them for allowable costs plus a 7.5 percent profit. For-profit hospitals and nonprofit nursing homes demanded, and got, the same deal. Before long, hospital supply companies were charging hospitals five times the regular price for everyday items such as scissors and furniture.[41] Doctors also profited handsomely under Part B. The insurance companies administering the program were supposed to monitor physicians' fees to make sure they were reasonable, but more than two years after Medicare began operating, fourteen major carriers still hadn't set up procedures to do so. Before Medicare, doctors typically charged what they thought a patient could afford; now, many of them were charging the government as much as they possibly could. "I am very glad to do charity work for my patients, but I certainly do not regard the federal government as an object of charity," one doctor remarked.[42]

Efforts in the 1970s and 1980s

BY THE EARLY 1970S, health-care costs were spiraling out of control and millions of people under 65 still didn't have insurance. When Massachusetts Senator Edward M. Kennedy became chairman of the Senate Health Subcommittee in 1971, he used the position—and his celebrity—to promote national health insurance. Senator Kennedy held hearings around the country, attracting fawning press coverage, and issued a report entitled, "The Health Care Crisis in America."[43] President Richard Nixon, wary of Senator Kennedy as a potential opponent in the 1972 presidential election, countered with his own health-care plan. Nixon's National Health Insurance Partnership Act aimed to preserve the private insurance market while requiring employers to either cover their workers or make payments into a government insurance fund. This "employer mandate" was endorsed by the Washington Business Group on Health, which was comprised of two hundred corporations, and the National Leadership Coalition for Health Care Reform, which included executives from Chrysler, Bethlehem Steel, Lockheed, Safeway, Xerox, and Georgia Pacific.[44]

But the Nixon presidency was soon consumed by the Watergate scandal, and Senator Kennedy's attempt to fashion a compromise national health insurance bill that preserved a role for private insurers ended up pleasing no one. The AMA and the National Federation of Independent Business denounced it as socialized medicine, and the AFL-CIO viewed it as a sellout.[45] In his first address to Congress after succeeding Nixon, President Gerald Ford urged lawmakers to approve a national health insurance bill, but President Ford's short tenure was dominated by high inflation and other economic woes.

Jimmy Carter also focused on inflation when he became president in 1977. Even though he had supported universal coverage during his campaign, President Carter decided that his first foray into health care would be an attempt to rein in costs, not expand coverage. In the previous decade, the consumer price index had increased by 79.7 percent, while hospital costs had risen 237 percent. President Carter proposed an across-the-board cap on hospital charges that would limit annual increases to one-and-a-half times any rise in the consumer price index, with an overall ceiling of 9 percent. But hospitals and the business community lobbied fiercely against the measure, and it never made it out of the Senate Finance Committee.[46]

Eventually, President Carter unveiled a plan to expand coverage: a compromise forged with Senator Kennedy that would have guaranteed health insurance for everyone while preserving a role for the private sector. But the plan's prospects suffered a crushing blow when President Carter dismissed his point man

on health issues, Joseph Califano, along with the rest of his cabinet in 1979 in an attempt to give his administration a fresh
start. In November of that year, the Iranian hostage crisis began
and health reform fell by the wayside. In 1980, Ronald Reagan
was elected president on a promise to limit government, not expand it. Washington wouldn't seriously consider universal coverage again until the early 1990s.

Why did national interest in universal coverage erode in
the 1980s? Many of those who had been fighting for national
health insurance viewed Medicare and Medicaid as a prelude,
merely the first steps toward covering everybody. But some
health economists believe the existence of those programs actually made it more difficult to attract support for a national
health insurance plan. Stanford economists Alain C. Enthoven
and Victor R. Fuchs have noted that without Medicare and
Medicaid, the percentage of uninsured people in 2005 would
have been more than 25 percent, instead of 16 percent. With
Medicare and Medicaid, more than 60 percent of the uninsured are under age 35. Without those programs, a huge portion of the uninsured would be elderly and poor, and there
would be stronger political pressure from their relatives and
financially strapped state and local governments.[47]

That is not to say that Americans were satisfied with their
health-care system in the 1980s. From the time I became a
member of the U.S. House of Representatives in 1979, the
open-door meetings I hosted in South Dakota were filled with
people eager to share their health-care horror stories with me.
The challenges they talked about then were remarkably similar
to the ones we are grappling with today. Some couldn't get in

surance because they had pre-existing conditions; others were struggling to pay for prescribed drugs.

Meanwhile, the employers who were paying many of the bills began taking a closer look at what they were being charged. Between 1970 and 1982, a period when the country's gross domestic product grew by 208 percent, employer spending on health benefits increased 700 percent. Why, employers wondered, did patients stay in the hospital for days after relatively simple procedures? Were all those expensive tests really necessary? And why did hospitals pay $19 for a box of Kleenex that cost 49 cents at Kmart?[48] The answer is that doctors and hospitals had little reason to care about costs. Hospitals considered doctors to be their clients, and doctors made the decisions about how to care for patients. They decided whom to admit to the hospital, how long to keep them there, and which tests to run. Doctors, bound by the Hippocratic Oath, had no reason to know or care about the cost of what they ordered. Hospitals were happy to earn as much money as possible by performing every test and procedure imaginable. Patients with insurance didn't pay much attention either, since they weren't paying the bills, and their main concern was getting well.[49] State taxes on insurance premiums and state rules mandating that all policies include certain services also affected the cost of coverage. By the mid-1980s, there were more than 690 mandates, requiring coverage of everything from wigs to podiatry. In many cases, it was the providers of the service, rather than patients, who lobbied for mandates.[50] Many smaller businesses had relied on Blue Cross plans with community-rating systems to hold down costs, but an increasing number of those plans were abandoning community rating in favor of the underwriting strategies of their commercial competitors.[51]

Some large corporations began acting on their own to contain costs. In 1978, when Lee Iacocca took the helm at the floundering Chrysler Corporation, he was amazed to find that the automaker paid more for health care, about $600 million annually, than it did for steel and rubber. The cost of health care was adding about $600 to each car.[52] Iacocca asked his old friend Joe Califano, recently fired by President Carter, to help him cut costs. Califano's first step was to conduct an audit of the company's medical expenses, and the results were shocking: He found that dermatologists were getting twice as much insurance money as general practitioners, and 25 percent more than chest surgeons. Chrysler workers and their dependents were staying twice as long in the hospital after normal vaginal births as the national average, and some podiatrists were working on only one toe during each visit to maximize their payments. Iacocca and Chrysler began requiring the use of generic drugs, found lower-priced laboratories to run tests, and pressured physicians to lower their prices. The company also launched a hospital admission screening program and created a "preferred provider" plan.[53]

Other large companies with unionized workers imitated Chrysler, while those without unions forced their employees to pay higher deductibles, higher co-payments, and a portion of premiums. Some firms also restricted or eliminated payments for expensive diseases such as cancer and AIDS.[54]

But these steps yielded only limited savings, so many employers resurrected a Nixon-era idea that had lain dormant for nearly a decade: managed care. Under the traditional "fee-for-service" model, the patient chooses the doctor, the doctor chooses the course of treatment, and the insurance company pays the bill. With no resource constraint, the natural inclination to do more, even if it wasn't worth it, prevailed. This attitude, combined with the steady arrival of new, expensive technologies, caused U.S. health spending to increase rapidly through the 1980s, from 8.9 percent of the GDP in 1980 to 13.6 percent of the GDP in 1993.[55]

Under managed care, patients are restricted to a network of approved doctors and hospitals, and a third party—a managed-care firm—to coordinate care and financing. The doctors and hospitals in a network agree to charge less for their services in exchange for a steady flow of patients, and patients that venture outside the network have to pay more. Because managed-care plans get paid the same amount for their healthiest and sickest enrollees, they have an incentive to keep costs down to keep profits up. Ideally, this promotes aggressive prevention and management of disease.

Initially, it worked. As more and more employers shifted to managed care, and saved significant sums as a result, there was hope that the United States had finally figured out how to curb its runaway health spending. In 1991 the editorial page of *The New York Times*, a longtime advocate for national health insurance, suggested that private managed care rather than public policy makers should lead the way:

Congressional leaders have proposed grandiose plans to provide universal, affordable coverage. But their proposals threaten widespread dislocations, and have triggered paralyzing opposition. But there's no need to depend on Congress. On the contrary, far from Capitol Hill, major corporations are moving to adopt cost-effective managed care plans, like Health Maintenance Organizations. The movement would become a national rush except for road-blocks thrown up by Federal and state laws. Thus there is one simple, powerful and effective step for Congress to take: Get legal obstacles out of the way. . . . [56]

During the 1980s, HMO enrollment grew fourfold, from 9.1 million in mid-1980 to 36.5 million at the end of 1990. By the beginning of the 1990s, 15 percent of U.S. residents were members of HMOs, and about 33 percent of insured employ-ees were in either an HMO or a preferred provider organiza-tion (PPO). Over half of all office-based doctors were affiliated with at least one HMO in 1990.[57]

A decade later, in the later 1990s, the aggressive cost-cutting prompted a backlash. Critics complained that managed care took medical decisions out of the hands of doctors and put them in the hands of clerks who favored the cheapest treatment over the best treatment. Managed-care companies forced some people to give up their trusted family physician for one in a net-work, and barred other patients from seeing specialists who might have helped them. Many desperately ill patients filed law-suits against managed-care companies to force them to pay for unproven but promising procedures that might save their lives. Doctors, outraged by the encroachment on their authority, also sued managed-care companies and lobbied state and federal lawmakers to curb their power. They pressured HMOs to make their coverage decisions public, and won rulings barring nonphysicians from denying care ordered by a physician. Virginia and Rhode Island approved laws permitting outside reviewers to evaluate HMO challenges to special referrals, and in New York, managed-care companies were ordered to reimburse patients for consultations with doctors outside the network. Three states cracked down on managed-care companies for refusing to pay for emergency room care.[58] But in the late 1980s and early 1990s, managed care was still considered a private-sector panacea.

Meanwhile, Republican Presidents Reagan and George H. W. Bush virtually ignored health care, and it hardly figured in the 1988 presidential campaign between then Vice President Bush and Massachusetts Governor Michael Dukakis. Nevertheless, during the 1980s the forces that would put the issue back on the national agenda were slowly building. Despite employers' cost-cutting efforts, health-care spending continued to climb rapidly, and economists were beginning to draw a connection between spiraling medical costs and stagnant wages. After decades of steady growth, the percentage of insured Americans began to decline, and by 1991 about 36 million people were without coverage. Aggressive underwriting practices and the advent of managed care made people feel insecure about the reliability of their coverage.

The Health Reform Debate
of the Early 1990s

THE ECONOMIC RECESSION of 1990–1991 and the surprising outcome of a U.S. Senate election in Pennsylvania sent these undercurrents rushing to the surface. As the recession deepened, many U.S. companies shed employees, and thousands of managerial and white-collar workers got their first taste of life without health insurance. I recall remarking to my staff during this time that health care seemed to be an increasingly urgent concern for the people I encountered in South Dakota and around the country. It didn't seem to matter what party people belonged to—Democrat or Republican, people were demanding that Congress do something.

During this period I was cochair of the Senate Democratic Policy Committee, and Senate Majority Leader George Mitchell asked me to take the lead in crafting a Democratic agenda for the 102nd Congress. In early 1991, I visited each Democratic office to survey senators' views and to collect ideas.

I remember being struck by the remarkable consistency of the recommendations—everybody wanted health-care reform to be near or at the top of our agenda. Senator after senator recounted tales that were nearly identical to what I was hearing from South Dakotans. All of us had hundreds, if not thousands, of constituents who had become victims of the system, people who couldn't get the care they needed or couldn't pay for it once they had gotten it. The senators I spoke to wanted to learn more. They wanted to meet the experts. They wanted Democratic leaders to devote time to understanding the health-care crisis, and to expend political capital to solve it. The senators believed the time was ripe for another reform effort.

Our political intuition was fortified by public opinion polls. In late 1991, opinion analysts Robert Blendon and Karen Donelan noted that many Americans "express fear of losing all or part of their health benefits in our employment-based system of health insurance" and that "60 percent of Americans worry they may not be adequately insured in the future."[59] In an influential article published in June 1991, in *The American Prospect*, sociologist Paul Starr argued that, "Thanks to the uncontrollable escalation of health costs and unraveling of private insurance, reform of the nation's health insurance system is being transformed, for the first time in recent decades, into a serious political concern for the middle class."[60]

> Few people under age sixty-five can be entirely confident today that they and their families will continue at all times to be protected by health insurance. They may be conservative and prudent, even vote Republican; still, if they develop a serious illness and lose their jobs or change employers, the

private insurance system cannot be counted on to protect them.[61]

One reader who was impressed by Starr's article was James Carville, the lead political consultant for a Democratic U.S. Senate candidate named Harris Wofford. Several months earlier, Wofford had been tapped by Pennsylvania's Democratic governor to finish the unexpired term of Republican Senator John Heinz, who had been killed in a plane crash. By the summer of 1991, it appeared that Wofford's Senate career would be exceedingly brief: In July, his own polls showed him trailing Republican Richard Thornburgh, a former Pennsylvania governor and U.S. Attorney General, by 47 points. Carville believed that Wofford's only chance of beating the patrician Thornburgh was to fashion a populist, pro-middle-class message that would appeal to average people who were struggling to pay their monthly bills.[62] In a meeting that August, pollster Mike Donilon presented survey results that helped the campaign hone its strategy. Donilon found that when people were told that Wofford favored national health insurance and Thornburgh did not, they supported Wofford 3 to 1. When they weren't told, the ratio was reversed.[63]

In September, the Wofford campaign ran a television ad featuring the candidate in an emergency room. "If criminals have the right to a lawyer, I think working Americans should have the right to a doctor ... I'm Harris Wofford, and I believe there is nothing more fundamental than the right to see a doctor when you're sick." Within weeks, Wofford had shaved Thornburgh's lead in half, a turnaround Donilon credited to the ad. On election day, Wofford cruised to victory with 55 percent of the vote, an astounding percentage in a state closely divided between Democrats and Republicans. According to Donilon, more than 30 percent of voters chose Wofford solely because of his position on health care.[64] Wofford's stunning victory convinced many politicians and interest groups that it was time to launch another drive for health-care reform. Dozens of health-care bills sprouted on Capitol Hill.

One of those bills was the American Health Security Act of 1992, my first proposal to overhaul our health-care system and the legislative marker I put down as the national debate loomed. Among its provisions were an employer mandate, purchasing pools, and a regulatory infrastructure modeled after the Federal Reserve System. I envisioned a new Federal Health Board that would make specific coverage decisions, but broadly speaking, every American would have had access to acute care, catastrophic care, primary and preventive care, long-term care, mental health services, home health care, and prescription drugs. It was, and remains, my view that our health-care system would function best in a public-private infrastructure similar to the one we have constructed for our monetary system. I will have much more to say about this model later.

In proposing my bill, I was entering a crowded field. Suddenly it seemed that every union, business organization, insurance company, and health-care advocacy group was pushing its own plan for overhauling the system. Most of the proposals fell into three basic categories: market-oriented reforms that would expand the private, individual insurance system; publicly financed "single-payer" plans that would cover everybody, with all medical bills paid by the federal government or some other public or quasi-public entity; and "play-or-pay" hybrids that would cover everybody by requiring employers to either insure their workers or contribute to the cost of their coverage through tax or assessment. President Bush, hoping to blunt the Democrats' momentum on the issue, unveiled a proposal in February 1992 that called for health-care tax credits and vouchers for low-income families, stricter oversight of insurance companies, and purchasing pools for small business. Seventy House members, backed by advocacy groups such as Citizen Action and the Consumers' Union, supported a single-payer plan that would be financed through taxes. Under that proposal, a variety of hospitals, doctors, and clinics—most of them private—would care for patients, but the federal government would be responsible for paying the bills. Senator Bob Kerry of Nebraska, who was seeking the Democratic nomination for president, advocated a single-payer plan that would be administered by the states.

Senator Wofford became the living symbol of the public's desire for change, and the authors of the competing plans vied for his favor. Despite the Pennsylvania senator's lack of seniority, his colleagues paraded to his office to pitch their proposals, hoping for his all-important imprimatur. I was one of the petitioners, and Senator Wofford agreed to cosponsor my bill.

As the 1992 election drew closer, the pay-or-play model emerged as the most promising approach. Liberals grumbled that the strategy would do nothing to hold down rising health-care costs, and that employers would be tempted to drop insurance coverage for their workers and dump them into an inferior insurance program. Conservatives warned that pay-or-play would lead to a single-payer system and socialized medicine. Nevertheless, pay-or-play represented middle ground in the increasingly rancorous health-care debate, and Democratic leaders seized it. We figured that if we could unite our party and put a pay-or-play bill on Bush's desk in 1992, the president would have to either move away from his purely market-driven approach, or wield his veto pen and hand a potent election year issue to us.[65]

But some in our party balked. Texas Senator Lloyd Bentsen, who was the chairman of the Senate Finance Committee, was not enthusiastic about advancing the pay-or-play bill, and sixty House Democrats in the Conservative Democratic Forum began looking for a path between President Bush's approach and the one backed by the Democratic leadership. Many of them became enamored of a strategy known as "managed competition," under which private insurers and health-care providers would compete for the business of "health-purchasing alliances," entities that would pool the buying power of businesses and individuals. While it wasn't my first choice, managed competition appeared to be one of the few options that could unite liberals and conservatives. Supporters of the idea said it would move the United States toward universal coverage, something progressives wanted, without expanding public insurance programs or burdening employers with a play-or-pay tax, which pleased conservatives. By the end of his successful campaign for president, Arkansas Governor Bill Clinton was a believer in managed competition—but he didn't start out that way.

When Governor Clinton announced his candidacy in Little Rock in October 1991, he proclaimed that "opportunity for all means reforming the health-care system to control costs, improve quality, expand preventive and long-term care, maintain consumer choice, and cover everybody." He continued:

> We don't have to bankrupt the taxpayers to do it. We do have to take on the big insurance companies and health-care bureaucracies and get some real cost-control into the system. I pledge to the American people that in the first year of a Clinton Administration we will present a plan to Congress and all the American people to provide affordable, quality health care for all Americans.[66]

Despite his impressive pledge, the Arkansas governor didn't yet have a plan to achieve it. From the beginning of his campaign, it was apparent that the single-payer approach wouldn't fit Governor Clinton's identity as a "New Democrat" who rejected "big government" policies. Beyond that, there were few specifics about the kind of health-care plan he favored. Several of his aides wanted to keep it that way; they didn't want the candidate to get bogged down in esoteric discussions of premiums and co-payments. But when Governor Clinton's Democratic rivals Senator Kerrey and former Massachusetts Senator Paul Tsongas laid out detailed plans in the weeks leading up to the New Hampshire primary, Governor Clinton chose to follow suit. In January 1992, he released an eight-page plan advocating a form of pay-or-play.[67]

After Governor Clinton became the nominee, however, President Bush pointed to the Democrat's pay-or-play plan as evidence that his opponent was just another "tax-and-spend" liberal in a New Democrat's clothing. Governor Clinton's campaign advisers worried that the president's charges were sticking, and in August and September of 1992 they began working on a new proposal that their candidate could unveil in a major September speech. Governor Clinton's embrace of managed competition wasn't purely political, however. An inveterate policy wonk, the Arkansas governor was naturally drawn to an elegant and intricate solution to the health-care puzzle—one that promised to combine the advantages of the three leading strategies without their weaknesses. Governor Clinton endorsed a carefully regulated version of managed competition: He wanted government subsidies to help the unemployed and small businesses purchase coverage through the regional alliances, and global budget caps to keep prices from rising too quickly. The Democratic nominee hoped this approach would please just about everybody. There would be no tax hike or new government health-care program; it held out the promise of affordable health coverage for every American; and it would preserve the private system while promoting managed care and other cost-cutting strategies.

By the time Governor Clinton adopted it, managed competition was being touted as the best approach by leading lights in academia and the media.[68] In a series of editorials in 1991, *The New York Times* strongly endorsed managed competition as the solution to America's health-care crisis. "A little-known system called managed competition offers the best way out. It can control costs, improve care, and guarantee coverage to every American," *The Times* opined in July of that year. "Unfettered competition would be insufficiently managed, leaving individuals, especially the chronically ill, at the mercy of providers. Government insurance would be insufficiently competitive, suppressing quality improvements. The best answer remains: Managed competition."[69] On September 24, the Democratic candidate laid out his new health-care plan at Merck Pharmaceuticals in Rahway, New Jersey. Without mentioning the term "managed competition," Governor Clinton portrayed his plan as "a private system. It is not pay-or-play. It does not require new taxes." He said his goal was "personal choice, private care, private insurance, private management, but a national system to put a lid on costs, to require insurance reforms, to facilitate partnerships between business, government, and health-care providers."[70] Governor Clinton won the three-way presidential race with only 42 percent of the vote. But with Democratic majorities in both the House and the Senate, many hoped that he could finally break the decades-old health-care impasse.

The Health Security Act's Birth and Death

CANDIDATE CLINTON HAD promised to send Congress a health-care plan within a hundred days of taking office, so his team began working on a proposal during the two-and-a-half month transition period. Just days after the inauguration, soon-to-be presidential aide Ira Magaziner submitted a twenty-three-page roadmap designed to produce a bill by May 1993. Magaziner called for the creation of an "Interagency Health-Care Task Force" broken into smaller "working groups" that would wrestle with specific issues, such as financing, cost control, and long-term care. He stressed that the task force, which would be comprised mainly of government officials, would reach out to every group with a stake in the health-care debate and keep in close contact with key congressional committees, governors, and mayors. The new president signed off on the task force and tapped First Lady Hillary Rodham Clinton to chair it. Magaziner would be responsible for running its day-to-day operations.

Magaziner had envisioned a task force of ninety-eight people—mostly administration officials from various agencies and congressional aides who worked for relevant committees. But the White House congressional liaison staff convinced Magaziner to allow all of the Democratic House and Senate members to assign staffers to the project. Cabinet agencies sent more people than were requested, and there were numerous health policy experts, academics, and physicians who participated as consultants or temporary government employees.[71] Eventually, the task force membership swelled to more than 630 people, broken down into thirty-four working groups. Magaziner presided over hours-long meetings known as "toll-gates," where the working groups presented policy recommendations on their particular subject areas. The result, Magaziner jokingly acknowledged, was "managed chaos."[72] The task force grew so large that those who weren't invited to participate were incensed at being snubbed. At the same time, it failed to solicit the views of the people who mattered most: the committee chairmen and other congressional leaders who would determine the fate of reform.

Despite the unwieldy size of the task force, the White House communications wanted the group's deliberations kept secret. The goal was to avoid publicizing preliminary proposals that might never win the president's approval. With so many people involved, however, it was impossible to prevent leaks. In retrospect, the administration might have assuaged the public's fears and managed news coverage by keeping key reporters in the loop. Instead, its secrecy policy made it possible for ill-informed or disgruntled members of the task force to leak inaccurate information to the press. The White House ended up with the worst of both worlds: The secrecy edict was a public-relations disaster, and it did nothing to prevent a constant stream of stories about ideas and proposals that weren't fully baked.

As promised, Magaziner's task force disbanded in May 1993. It handed its proposals to several smaller teams of administration officials, who were charged with performing tasks such as calculating the costs, putting final decisions into legislative language, and plotting political strategy. Their work nearly ground to a halt during the summer, as the administration concentrated on passing President Clinton's first budget. The president didn't want to finalize any financial decisions on health care until that battle was over. After his budget cleared the Senate by a single vote in early August, President Clinton turned his attention to health care, and by September 7 a few copies of the "Working Group Draft" were sent to Capitol Hill for comment. Overall, the plan hewed closely to what Clinton the candidate had proposed at Merck Pharmaceuticals during the campaign: It called for universal coverage, mostly financed through an employer mandate, and competition between private plans, regulated by government, to keep costs down.[73]

The atmosphere on Capitol Hill was electric, and everybody was eager to get started. To get members of Congress up to speed on the complexities of the health-care issue, I helped organize a "Health-Care University" on the Hill. Majority Leader George Mitchell and I feared that many of us weren't prepared to make the complicated decisions on the road to reform. To equip lawmakers for the journey ahead, we brought some of the best minds in the country to Washington to conduct workshops on various aspects of the health-care issue. We began the day with a session in Statuary Hall, where the First Lady gave us an overview of the president's plan. Then more than three hundred of us split up for break-out sessions. *The Washington Post* described the scene: "Like students, many members of Congress roamed the hilltop campus yesterday clutching yellow textbooks and looking for signs directing them to rare Monday classes, when many of them usually would have been in their home states."[74]

Like Truman nearly a half-century before, President Clinton formally presented his plan in a speech before a joint session of Congress on September 22, 1993. I saw the president in an antechamber in the Capitol shortly before his address, and he seemed to be uncharacteristically nervous. He was sweating, and appeared to be preoccupied. Perhaps he was overwhelmed by the moment—I know a lot of us were. For many of us, it was a night of incredible excitement and anticipation. There was a sense that we were making history. Many Democrats, including senators such as Ted Kennedy, who had worked on the issue for years, believed the country was finally on the verge of creating a new national health-care system.

President Clinton came through with an impassioned performance, one that was all the more impressive because the TelePrompTer displayed the wrong speech for several minutes and he had to begin speaking without the text:

> This health care system of ours is badly broken and it is
> time to fix it. Despite the dedication of literally millions of

talented health care professionals, our health care is too uncertain and too expensive, too bureaucratic and too wasteful. It has too much fraud and too much greed. At long last, after decades of false starts, we must make this our most urgent priority: giving every American health security, health care that can never be taken away, health care that is always there. That is what we must do tonight.

During the speech the president displayed a freshly minted red, white, and blue "health security" card that he held aloft as he promised that his plan would cover each and every American. "With this card, if you lose your job or you switch jobs, you're covered," he declared. "If you leave your job to start a small business, you're covered. If you're an early retiree, you're covered." And he concluded his appeal with stirring words that invoked the New Deal and the sweep of history.

It's hard to believe that once there was a time—even in this century—when retirement was nearly synonymous with poverty, and older Americans died in our streets. That is unthinkable today because over a half century ago Americans had the courage to change—to create a Social Security System that ensures that no Americans will be forgotten in their later years. I believe that forty years from now, our grandchildren will also find it unthinkable that there was a time in our country when hardworking families lost their homes and savings simply because their child fell ill, or lost their health coverage when they changed jobs. Yet, our grandchildren will only find such things unthinkable tomorrow, if we have the courage to change today. This is our chance. This is our journey. And, when our work is done, we will know that we have answered the call of history and met the challenge of our times.

As President Clinton exited the Capitol and strode toward his waiting limousine, he asked some of us who were accompanying him, "How did I do?" Our collective answer was, "You did very well, Mr. President." I added, "It was a home run!" We weren't alone in our assessment: The media gave the president rave reviews, and polls showed the American people were similarly enthusiastic.

The reaction to President Clinton's speech was uniformly positive—but it might have been surpassed by Hillary Clinton's reception when she testified before five congressional committees less than a week later. The First Lady fielded complicated questions, without notes, for hours. She remained cool and poised throughout, disarming the few hostile questioners with deference, flattery, and self-deprecating humor. In the Senate, Republican Jim Jeffords of Vermont publicly endorsed President Clinton's plan after hearing the First Lady's testimony, telling her, "I am pleased to be the first. I am absolutely confident I will not be the last." Another Republican, John Danforth of Missouri, said, "We will pass a law next year."[75]

The First Lady's virtuoso performance made it easy to forget that many were skeptical when President Clinton tapped his wife as leader of the health reform effort. Hillary Clinton hadn't been elected, and she didn't have an extensive healthcare background. But by the time she was finished testifying at those hearings, even her most ardent opponents had to admit she knew her stuff.

How powerful was the health-care issue in the summer and fall of 1993? Consider what twenty-three Republican senators, including Minority Leader Robert Dole of Kansas, were proposing at the time. Like President Clinton, they wanted to prohibit insurers from denying coverage on the basis of pre-existing conditions. Their proposal would have guaranteed a certain level of coverage to everyone buying a policy, and encouraged individuals and businesses to join purchasing cooperatives to maximize their market clout—just like President Clinton. The White House and the Republican senators also agreed on the need to promote competition by giving consumers more information on the price and effectiveness of medical procedures. The Senate Republicans opposed an employer mandate, but they hoped to achieve universal coverage with a mandate on individuals to purchase insurance. Even in the House, where moderate Republicans were an endangered species, the desire for reform appeared to be strong. More than one hundred House Republicans endorsed a plan setting strict limits on pre-existing condition exclusions and curbing insurers' ability to charge different premiums for different small businesses. Their proposal also would have allowed employers to band into large purchasing cooperatives, and would have given financial help to low-income people who wanted to buy into Medicaid or other state-designated insurance plans. Less than a week before the president's speech to Congress, *The Washington Post* noted that "after a decade of deal-crushing disagreements between Congress and the

White House over health-care reform, a consensus on the broad outlines for restructuring the U.S. system appears to be jelling."[76]

As the Clintons boarded Air Force One for a trip to California on October 3, it seemed that health-care reform was unstoppable. Polls showed strong and rising support for the president's plan, and the administration planned a slew of events to promote the cause. There were rumblings of opposition from the National Federation of Independent Business (NFIB) and the Health Insurance Association of America (HIAA) but the prospects for reform were bright. Then disaster struck: While in the air, the president was told that eighteen U.S. Army Rangers had been killed in a firefight with warlord clan factions in Somalia. Mobs of Somalis had dragged the corpses of U.S. soldiers through the streets, and one injured helicopter pilot was being held hostage. President Clinton had to cut short his trip, and once he returned to Washington he canceled all his health-care events to deal with the crisis. Then foreign policy fires erupted in Haiti and Russia. As a result, all but one health-care event in October had to be scrapped. The succession of crises hurt President Clinton's popularity, delayed the bill's introduction, and gave opponents of his plan valuable time to mobilize.[77] Right after the president's speech, a *Washington Post*/ABC News poll showed that the percentage of people with a favorable view of his plan exceeded the percentage of people who didn't like it by 32 points. Three weeks later, the gap had shrunk to 12 points.[78]

On October 27, the Clintons came to Statuary Hall to regain the momentum they had lost during the previous month.

To highlight their desire to work with Republicans, they invited House Minority Leader Bob Michel of Illinois, who was a throwback to a less rancorous, less partisan congressional era. But instead of offering up the usual bromides about working together to reach shared goals, the Republican leader lit into the president's plan, proclaiming that the coming debate was about whether Americans would "embark on an uncharted course of government-run medicine."[79]

The size and complexity of the president's bill, which arrived on Capitol Hill in its final form on November 20, worried both Democrats and Republicans. At 1,342 pages, it was long and highly technical. Reporters had a hard time translating the bill into plain English for readers and viewers because they didn't understand it themselves. Even some in the administration shuddered at the scale of the proposal. Bob Boorstin of the White House communications office said he and his colleagues counted more than ninety new councils, commissions, and other bodies that would be created by the plan. "We came up with such a big, fat, ugly bill that was such an easy target," Boorstin said. "We created a target the size of Philadelphia."[80] In his own postmortem, Starr wrote that President Clinton's plan was so huge, and included so many new regulations, it "caused sympathetic groups in the business community and opinion leaders in the media to think twice about support for reform."

> Because we had failed to edit the plan down to its essentials and find familiar ways to convey it, many people

couldn't understand what we were proposing. There were too many parts, too many new ideas, even for many policy experts to keep straight.[81]

Once President Clinton's legislation was introduced, Representative Michel's top aide hosted regular Monday morning meetings where GOP staffers coordinated strategy with lobbyists dedicated to derailing the bill. Many groups sent lobbyists to those meetings, but the HIAA and the NFIB emerged as the leaders of the burgeoning anti-Clinton plan coalition. HIAA represented about 270 small and medium-size insurers (the largest insurance companies, which had shifted their focus to running their own managed-care networks, had recently left the group). It was headed by Willis D. Gradison, a sixty-four-year-old former Republican congressman from Cincinnati who was well-liked on both sides of the aisle. Gradison struck a reasonable tone, but he argued that President Clinton's plan might force many of his members out of business. HIAA members were afraid that the regional alliances in the president's bill would bar some smaller insurers from the marketplace. They also opposed the plan's premium growth constraints and feared they would be forced to use community rating.[82] John Motley, NFIB's chief lobbyist, prided himself on a take-no-prisoners approach. President Clinton's employer mandate was anathema to the businesses Motley represented: Sixty percent of them had fewer than ten employees, and only a fourth of those firms provided health-care coverage. Requiring them to do so, NFIB argued, would be a crushing financial burden.[83]

Both groups quickly realized that traditional lobbying techniques—namely, cajoling congressmen and their aides behind closed doors—wouldn't work in this particular fight. President Clinton had taken his case to the American people; HIAA and NFIB would have to do the same. In its grassroots campaign, HIAA hired field operatives in six states whose lawmakers were expected to be swing votes, and recruited ground troops from member companies' networks of employees, managers, and agents. The field directors focused on finding "grass tops," community leaders and people with personal links to members of Congress, and connected them with Capitol Hill via phone and fax when it was time for a crucial vote. By the end of its campaign, HIAA had generated more than 450,000 phone calls, visits, and letters to Congress.[84]

HIAA also sowed public doubts about President Clinton's plan with its famous "Harry and Louise" television ads, which depicted a forty-something, middle-class white couple expressing fears about what the president's proposal would mean for them. HIAA only ran the ads in Washington, New York, and the districts of key congressmen, but the White House's furious reaction to the spots prompted widespread media coverage. When the Clintons spoofed the ads at the annual dinner of the Gridiron Club, an organization of Washington newspaper reporters, they gave Harry and Louise even more publicity. The ads also were a potent fundraising tool for HIAA: By the time the debate was over, the group had raised and spent about $50 million, $30 million more than its typical annual operating budget.[85]

NFIB, according to Motley, launched "the largest single

focused grassroots lobbying campaign we have ever done." The group used frequent "Fax Alerts" and "Action Alerts" to brief its members on President Clinton's plan and arm them to do their own lobbying. NFIB also pressured key lawmakers by sending mass mailings to their constituents, and by holding seminars in their home states that highlighted how the president's plan would harm local businesspeople. Every two months, NFIB polled its 600,000 members on their health-care opinions and sent the results to congressional offices. The group reached out aggressively to the media, offering up small-business people to newspaper reporters and talk radio hosts.[86]

My constituents were increasingly confused. They wanted health care to be fixed, but they were beginning to believe the messages that reform opponents were sending. Harry and Louise registered with them. For more than a year, the voices of the people harmed by the current system had dominated the debate. Now they were being drowned out by special interests.

Undoubtedly, the enemies of President Clinton's plan mounted a skillful campaign against it. But their cause was helped greatly by the actions—and inaction—of those who backed the bill. Unions and some other liberal groups rewarded the president's proponents in Congress with substantial support, but their overall lobbying effort was anemic compared to the exertions of the other side. The Center for Public Integrity estimated that opponents spent more than $100 million to defeat health-care reform, while supporters spent only $15 million. Many union members, still seething over the president's support of the North American Free Trade Agreement (NAFTA), weren't eager to come to his aid on health care. President Clinton lamented the fact that even though the groups aligned against his bill were outnumbered by those in favor of it, the opponents fought with far more intensity.[87] Starr concluded that "Harry and Louise" and grassroots lobbying "helped to create public anxiety and political paralysis, but their influence is easily exaggerated."

> Several of the key interest groups were actually less hostile to reform than in any prior battle over health insurance since the 1930s. The problem was not so much that the opponents had more resources, but that the supporters could not mobilize theirs. While the antagonists had great clarity of purpose, the groups backing reform suffered from multiple and complex fractures and were unable to unite.[88]

The length and detail of President Clinton's proposal was part of the problem. In my experience, the challenge of passing a bill is directly proportional to its size. Many groups were generally sympathetic to the president's plan, but in 1,300-plus pages they were bound to find a few things they didn't like. Aetna, MetLife, Cigna, Prudential, and Travelers withdrew from HIAA because the group failed to back health-care reform, and they supported the principle of managed competition. But they worried that the purchasing alliances would end up with too much regulatory authority, and feared the creation of a national health board that could cap prices. Large manufacturers straining under the financial burden of covering their workers and retirees were clamoring for reform, but they ended up abandoning the president's plan because they worried that its basic benefits package was too generous and its safeguards against lawsuits by employees were too weak. If they withheld their unqualified support, many groups figured, they would have some leverage when Congress hashed out the final details. The complexity of the president's plan also made it hard for supportive groups to mobilize. White House aide Mike Lux explained the problem in a December 1993 memo to the president:

> Because of the complexity of our bill and the huge levels of misinformation and misunderstanding about it, supportive groups are having to devote enormous amounts of resources to educating their *activists*, let alone their members. This huge educational process is slowing down the groups' ability to move people into action. Until they get ahead of the curve on this process, grassroots pressures on our side will be relatively sparse.[89]

Meanwhile, with difficulty, we tried to move the legislation through Congress. Democrats controlled both houses of Congress, but GOP lawmakers were far more unified in opposition to President Clinton's plan than the majority party was in favor of it. On the left, a single-payer bill authored by Representative Jim McDermott and Senator Paul Wellstone had a total of ninety congressional cosponsors and the backing of the American Federation of State, County and Municipal

Employees, the Communications Workers of America, the United Mine Workers of America, Consumers Union, the Gray Panthers, and various public health and mental health advocacy groups. The White House bowed to the power of this coalition by committing to universal coverage, and by promising to allow states to implement single-payer plans if they wished. Single-payer supporters knew they didn't have the votes to enact a full-fledged version of their bill. Nevertheless, they kept the president at arm's length and continued to promote single-payer principles through the spring of 1994, hoping to extract concessions from the White House. Instead, they helped to splinter the fragile coalition in favor of universal coverage.[90]

The president also faced a challenge on his right flank. Dozens of conservative Democrats backed a bill, proposed by Tennessee Representative Jim Cooper, which would have created a system of market-oriented managed competition, without a guarantee of universal coverage. The Cooper plan had Clinton-style alliances, but it did not require all employers to insure their workers, and did not include the premium growth limitations that critics labeled "government price controls." By late 1993 and early 1994, Cooper's "Clinton Lite" strategy had garnered the support of powerful business, insurance, and health-industry interests. The Cooper plan and its boosters undermined the president's desire to portray his own plan as centrist.[91] My own view of the Cooper bill was that it was somewhat better than what we had, but far short of what we needed. I remained optimistic that in spite of rising opposition and a divided Democratic party, we would ultimately prevail with something much closer to President Clinton's model.

President Clinton and the First Lady tried to use their bully pulpits to keep the reform effort moving forward. But while they were eloquent in outlining the problem, they seemed to be far less successful when it came to promoting their plan for solving it. We had one of the best political communicators in history on our side, and yet we were far less effective than our opponents were in getting our message across. That shouldn't have been the case.

A *Wall Street Journal*/NBC News poll conducted in March 1994, as support for the president's plan flagged, offered a fascinating glimpse into the communication problem that vexed the White House throughout the debate. Forty-five percent of respondents said they opposed the president's proposal, up from 39 percent in January 1994 and 18 percent in September 1993, just after President Clinton's triumphant speech. But when the poll participants were read a brief description of the major provisions of the bill, without the "Clinton" label, 76 percent of them said it had either "a great deal of appeal" or "some appeal." Unlabeled descriptions of four other plans pending in Congress didn't generate nearly the same level of enthusiasm. "The White House should find this both satisfying and sobering," said Peter Hart, one of the two pollsters who conducted the survey for the news organizations. "Satisfying because the basic ideas which they've drawn up are the right ideas" in the view of many people, but "sobering because they clearly have communicated very little to the public, and in that respect have ceded too much to the interest groups."[92]

By the summer of 1994, health-care reform was hopelessly bogged down. Democrats were divided. Those Republicans who had been open to the idea of reform were beginning to sense that they could seize control of both houses of Congress in the fall, and most of them weren't in any mood to compromise and give President Clinton and the Democrats a victory. Some Republicans who had been lamenting the health-care crisis for decades now denied there was one. GOP leaders were embracing the "scorched-earth" policy that Republican strategist William Kristol had laid out in a five-page memo he faxed to conservative leaders. His advice: Resist the Clinton plan in any form.

I was among those Democrats who wanted to hold reform opponents accountable by forcing a vote on the president's proposal. But I was in the minority; most of my colleagues were ready to let the issue die a quiet death. With the elections fast approaching, many people on our side of the aisle didn't want a vote on the Clinton plan any more than the Republicans did. The president was increasingly unpopular, and many Democrats weren't eager to be associated with him. I remember that Majority Leader Mitchell was deeply frustrated with his inability to move the bill.

At the end of the summer, Senators Mitchell and Kennedy, and moderate Republican Senator John Chafee of Rhode Island made a last-ditch attempt to craft a bipartisan bill that would expand coverage without enacting comprehensive reform. But the trio was unable to secure the sixty votes they needed to stop

a filibuster in the Senate. Meanwhile, House Minority Leader
Newt Gingrich used a mid-September meeting with President
Clinton to make a not-so-veiled threat: If the president con-
tinued to push health-care reform, Minority Leader Gingrich
made it clear, Republicans would kill the pending General
Agreement on Tariffs and Trade (GATT).

On September 26, Senator Mitchell officially pulled the
plug at a news conference in the Capitol. In a ten-paragraph
statement, he explained that he just didn't have the votes to
pass a health-care bill, so it made no sense to continue. In the
end, he said, "the combination of the insurance industry on
the outside and a majority of Republicans on the inside
proved to be too much to overcome."[93] President Clinton,
who was in New York that day to address the United Nations
General Assembly, released a written statement. "I am very
sorry that this means Congress isn't going to reform health
care this year," the statement read. "But we are not giving up
on our mission to cover every American and to control
health-care costs. This journey is far, far from over."[94]

A little over a year had passed since President Clinton had
launched his drive for health-care reform with his masterful
speech to Congress. At that time, the forces arrayed behind the
president, both inside and outside Congress, appeared to be so
numerous and powerful that many believed success was a fore-
gone conclusion. Everybody was in favor of health-care reform.
Everybody agreed that the system had to change. But when it
came down to the details, few groups were willing to tolerate
provisions that might harm them, to swallow new regulations,
or to sacrifice some profits for the greater good. Instead of

seeing the broad picture, each stakeholder focused on its own narrow interests and dug in for battle. The result is that the great health-care debate of the early 1990s expired with barely a whimper.

Incremental Reform

CONGRESS DID TAKE some modest steps to expand coverage following the demise of the Clinton plan. In 1996, Senators Edward Kennedy and Nancy Kassebaum, a respected Kansas Republican, coauthored the Health Insurance Portability and Accountability Act (HIPAA). Senators Kennedy and Kassebaum hoped to limit the situations under which insurance companies could deny coverage. Their original bill would have banned experience rating and made it more difficult for insurance companies to deny coverage because of a pre-existing condition. It also would have ensured that policy holders could renew their coverage, and guaranteed that new workers would be admitted to already covered groups. But HIAA vigorously opposed the plan. In the end, Congress approved a more limited measure that gave employees who lost their group coverage and exhausted their COBRA the right to convert these policies to individual coverage. The final version also barred insurers from charging different premiums for individuals within the same group, and forced insurers in the small group market to renew coverage for any group. It also allowed people to partially deduct the cost of long-term care insurance. Overall, however, HIPAA did not fulfill its authors' aim of preventing insurers from denying coverage to people because of their medical conditions.

In 1997, Congress took action to cover more children. Under the State Children's Health Insurance Program (SCHIP), the federal government allocated money to the states so they could insure low-income children, either by expanding Medicaid or launching a separate initiative. SCHIP sharply reduced the number of uninsured children. It also encouraged governors to expand coverage more broadly, and has been widely considered a success.

Despite those victories, the two postdebate developments that stand out for me were both disappointments. The first was our failure to approve a patients' bill of rights, despite its limited scope and strong bipartisan support for the idea. Passing a patients' bill of rights was my top priority when I became majority leader in June 2001, and both the Senate and House approved legislation. It would have ensured basic consumer protection to ensure access to health care in managed-care plans. Unfortunately, we could never hammer out the differences between the two proposals, in part due to the same old special-interest pressures.

The second disappointment was the Medicare Modernization Act, which Congress approved in 2003. Although the measure added a prescription drug benefit to Medicare for the first time, it was a huge handout to the drug and insurance companies and came at an extraordinary cost. Seniors' coverage has a gap in it—often called a "doughnut hole"—that leaves them vulnerable to high costs. Taxpayers' costs have been higher than originally thought. And Medicare's solvency is now threatened by overpayments to private insurers built into the legislation.

In short, few of the measures we managed to pass have lessened the health-care burden for some people, but they haven't come close to solving the broader problem. Others have made matters worse. And neglect is perhaps even more damaging. Our system is fundamentally flawed, and without fundamental change we can expect medical costs, and the number of people without insurance, to grow.

Part Three

WHAT
WENT WRONG
AND MODELS
FOR MAKING
IT RIGHT

For almost a century we have tried to reform our health-care system so that every American can get affordable, high-quality care. Despite the best efforts of skilled lawmakers, passionate advocates, and presidents from Truman to Clinton, we've failed. If we are to succeed next time, it is crucial to understand what went wrong, and to figure out how we can avoid the same pitfalls in the future. Certainly, the substance of the failed bills had something to do with their demise. But I think that ideological differences and disputes over policy weren't really to blame. After all, there is a general agreement on basic reform principles. The consensus in the middle of the political spectrum, among both Democrats and Republicans, is that we should create a public-private hybrid that preserves our private system within a strengthened public framework. So, if many of us agree on the broad outlines of a plan, if not the details, why haven't we been able to get it done?

I believe we have to look harder at the exceptional nature

of the health-care problem, and reconsider the political process we've followed in trying to solve it. The stakes are extraordinarily high in health care—literally life and death—and the issue is incredibly complex. The number of the stakeholders and special interests involved is extraordinarily large, and their influence is immense. Powerful and pervasive myths about the "success" of our system have helped reinforce the status quo. Given these obstacles, perhaps it isn't surprising that the traditional legislative process has failed to deliver. Yet, in similarly thorny areas, such as military base closures and monetary policy, we've gotten results by creating a decision-making process that is one step removed from Congress and the White House. In part three, I will argue that the health-care crisis calls for the same approach.

Barriers to Reform

IN THE SUMMER and fall of 1993, the question was *how* we would reform our health-care system, not *whether* we would do it. People were excited, and passage of a plan seemed inevitable. But a year after President Clinton's triumphant performance on Capitol Hill, the effort was declared dead. What happened? There are as many theories as there were pages in the president's plan.

To be sure, the substance of President Clinton's proposal—and its length, which made it a large target—helped seal its fate. The complicated employer mandate became a lightning rod, and was especially odious to small-business owners. The cap on premium increases infuriated insurers and probusiness Democrats. The benefits package was laid out in excruciating detail, allowing the left to pan it as too slim and the right to attack it as overly generous. There was much in the bill I would have changed—but I don't believe that the substance of the proposal was decisive in its defeat. After all, a decade later

Governors Mitt Romney of Massachusetts and Arnold Schwarzenegger of California, both Republicans, would adopt its basic structure.

Many argue, and I agree, that timing was a more important factor. In retrospect, we waited too long after President Clinton took office to mount a major push for reform. Some suggested that we speed up the process by attaching the health-care plan to the federal budget bill. That strategy would have put a time limit on the debate, and eliminated the possibility of a filibuster. But Robert Byrd of West Virginia, one of the Senate's longest-serving members, insisted that Senate rules precluded that approach. Senator Byrd's stand ensured that the health-care debate would be delayed; having ridden their "It's the economy, stupid" mantra to victory in the 1992 election, President Clinton and his advisers were convinced that the budget had to come first. The president's desire to get the North American Free Trade Agreement (NAFTA) through Congress bumped health care back even further. He believed he had to take on NAFTA before health care, because otherwise, opponents of the trade pact would have time to pick it apart. The White House's political strategy resulted in a hard-fought budget victory and passage of NAFTA, but it gave opponents of health-care reform an edge, according to Gradison of HIAA.

> We had lots of time to get geared up. It gave us a lot more time to refine our message, raise our money, do internal staffing changes, and have training sessions with members of our association as to what they could do with their hometowns and their editorial boards.[1]

The health-care debate might have played out differently if President Clinton had launched it in the spring of 1993, when he still had some momentum from his election victory. But to be fair, the timing of the debate wasn't entirely in his hands. The late Senator Patrick Moynihan of New York, who chaired the powerful Senate Finance Committee, wasn't eager to take up the president's bill. Senator Moynihan voiced doubts that the health-care system needed fixing, and urged the administration to tackle welfare reform instead. I was a member of the Finance Committee, and I talked to Majority Leader Mitchell many times about how we could move Senator Moynihan to a more supportive position and push the president's bill out of his committee. But Senator Moynihan believed the White House should have given the relevant committees a greater role in drafting the bill, and he was troubled by many of its provisions. He kept repeating that we had a health-care *financing* problem, not a health-care problem. He also argued that reform advocates were too divided, and that without greater unity behind the president's approach, the committee might vote against it. With more time, Senator Moynihan argued, we might yet attract some Republicans to the cause. President Clinton himself later mused that overhauling the welfare system earlier might have helped him build trust with the moderates he needed to succeed on health reform.

Sociologist Paul Starr, a member of the health-care task force, argued in a 1995 article that the White House wasted valuable time by trying to craft the perfect plan on its own, rather than bringing in congressional leaders almost immediately.

> The real problem was that time was spent developing a plan that should have been spent negotiating it; congressional negotiations did not get under way until the midterm elections were within spitting distance. Those who felt shut out responded predictably. On health care, the administration ignored the first rule of political cooperation, "In on the takeoff, in on the landing," which underlay other quieter and more successful legislative initiatives.[2]

Relying so heavily on the task force almost certainly contributed to the eventual defeat of the president's plan. The task force and its chaotic "tollgates" only bred resentment among the people who weren't invited to participate, and produced a "compromise" without the input of key stakeholders. In my view, the White House should have engaged congressional leaders in a more meaningful way at the very beginning, on both the substance of the bill and the strategy for passing it. What would an alternative path have looked like? Perhaps the Clinton administration should have turned to the Department of Health and Human Services, where political appointees and career bureaucrats could have worked together to draft a plan. As they proceeded, the HHS officials might have solicited the views of academics, congressional staffers, and interest groups. Political veterans in the White House could have assessed the plan's political feasibility. Then, before anything was finalized, HHS would have run it by congressional leaders and powerful interest groups to identify potential problems.[3]

Perhaps better timing and tactics would have produced a better result in the early 1990s. But I believe the roots of the failure run deeper, to the complexity of health care and questions of trust. Consider the complexity of the issues that would-be reformers have had to grapple with. For example, past health-care reform efforts often have bogged down over benefits. What medical services should the government, or private insurers, have to cover? This is a question that has flummoxed lawmakers, driven up cost estimates of the various reform schemes, and sparked the fiercest combat between powerful special interests. White House policy-makers and members of Congress aren't qualified to make those decisions. And every year, as technology advances, the decisions become more difficult to make.

Anyone who has been seriously ill knows how bewildering our labyrinthine health-care system can be. An American with an injury or illness is likely to encounter a wide array of providers, from emergency room doctors to nurse practitioners to primary care physicians to specialists, who aren't necessarily in contact with one another. Trying to navigate the system can be like taking a multiple-choice exam in a subject you've never studied. Do I really need this test, or is it a waste of money? Is this doctor prescribing the right course of treatment, or should I seek a second opinion? Then there is our confusing financing system, with its dizzying array of reimbursement rates and deductibles and coverage limits. How many average Americans truly understand it?

Because health care is so complex, special-interest experts have the upper hand in their dealings with lawmakers. Every program, no matter how small, has providers and patients determined to protect it. The drug industry often locks arms with patient advocates to ensure that a certain drug is covered by insurance, and this patient-provider pincer movement is extremely powerful. Doctors, hospitals, and insurers are important constituents for members of Congress, and they spend vast sums on lobbying. They have perfected what I call the "human shield" strategy: They inevitably argue that no change can be made without depriving a vulnerable person of health or wealth.

I saw how the complexity of health care can short-circuit political action as soon as I was elected to Congress in the late 1970s. As the first Vietnam-era veteran to serve on the House Veterans Committee, I took an early interest in the controversy over Agent Orange, the herbicide and defoliant used by the U.S. military in Vietnam that has been linked to certain cancers in veterans who were exposed to it, and to birth defects in their children. In the years after the war, the scientific evidence of Agent Orange's health effects mounted—but you wouldn't have known it if you were listening to the VA, the Pentagon, or the Centers for Disease Control and Prevention. Government studies were, at best, poorly executed, and at worst, intentionally undermined. Routinely, negative results were heralded, and positive results were downplayed. The government tried to discredit key independent research and touted its own incomplete or inaccurate studies as evidence that few, if any, veterans were harmed by Agent Orange. Congress, which along with the VA can designate service-related disabilities, was paralyzed. My overarching goal was to get veterans a fair hearing on their disability claims. They finally got it, after a decade of struggle, in 1991 when we passed a law designating the Institute of Medicine as an independent arbiter to evaluate the scientific and medical evidence.

Health care is an intensely personal, life-and-death issue; overhauling the system will have a profound effect on millions of individuals, every business that pays for benefits, and a giant sector of our economy. That is why the American people need to know that decisions on coverage and cost are being made for the public good, and aren't tainted by politics or special interests. The secrecy of the task force, the large scope of President Clinton's plan and its bureaucratic language, the special-interest war that erupted around it—all of these eroded people's trust. As the months passed without action, reform opponents succeeded in confusing and even frightening Americans about what change might mean. Eventually, many people decided they preferred the status quo, as flawed as it was. Issues of trust also figured in earlier failures, as opponents of reform were able to capitalize on people's fears and lack of knowledge about health care to stop change in its tracks.

Professional expertise and trustworthiness—these are qualities that Congress lacks when it comes to health care. But there is a way out of this predicament. In other areas where Congress has these deficiencies, we've delegated power to quasi-independent entities comprised of credible experts who are immune from political pressure. I believe health care calls for the same approach.

Models for Health Reform

CONSIDER THE BASE Realignment and Closure Commission (BRAC), which deals with an issue that would be difficult, if not impossible, for lawmakers to tackle. The Pentagon's decision to close about five hundred military bases after the Vietnam War left many lawmakers, especially Democrats, with a sour taste in their mouths. The closures led to massive job losses, and Democrats were convinced they were politically motivated, because most of the targeted bases were in their districts. In 1976, Congress retaliated by passing a law requiring a full environmental impact statement whenever a base was closed, effectively ending base closures for a dozen years.

The case of Loring Air Force Base in Maine was typical. Loring had been a vital outpost for B-52 bombers that could reach the Soviet Union from the U.S. mainland. But as newer aircraft and nuclear submarines assumed the B-52's defense role, the Pentagon decided it should downgrade Loring to a military airfield with a minimal crew. The required environmental review gave opponents time to mobilize, however, and they lobbied Congress and the Defense Department to reverse the decision. A "Save Loring Committee" was formed, and before long the Senate approved a bill prohibiting the downsizing of the base. The Pentagon was forced to back off.[4]

As the Cold War wound down in the late 1980s, an increasing number of lawmakers were willing to acknowledge that many military bases around the country were obsolete. Nevertheless, Congress was loath to close any of the bases because so many jobs depended on them. Whenever a certain base was singled out as superfluous and ripe for closure, the affected lawmaker would rally colleagues who had aging bases in their own districts, warning that they could be next. The result was a deadlock. In 1988, Congress and the Pentagon came up with BRAC as a solution. The former lawmakers and retired military officers on the commission work with experts at the Pentagon to craft a list of base closures and realignments. When they have compiled a list, they present it to the Secretary of Defense, who has to either accept or reject it without alteration. Finally, the list is submitted to Congress for a single up-or-down vote. In five rounds since 1988, BRAC has closed or shrunk dozens of bases and saved billions of dollars.

The BRAC process is as valiant an attempt as Congress has made to create a workable process of critical national decisions. But as successful as it has been since 1988, the latest BRAC round underscores the difficulty of keeping politics out of policy-making. I saw this process up close in South Dakota, where I fought against the closure of Ellsworth Air Force Base in the western part of our state. The process as overseen by the

Bush White House was an eye-opener, even for me. Despite the legal requirement to keep political considerations out of the final decision to close any base, the White House made Ellsworth's future a principal issue in my own campaign for re-election. That experience illustrates a fundamental challenge in health reform: To keep narrow and political interests from driving these important decisions, we need not just structural checks, but dramatically increased transparency.

BRAC isn't the only model. In other cases, Congress delegates authority to the White House. For example, the legislative branch is constitutionally responsible for negotiating international trade agreements, but it cedes this power, within certain guidelines, to the administration's trade negotiators. When an agreement has been reached, Congress votes yes or no on it. Without this "fast-track" system, lawmakers would be able to pick apart individual provisions of a deal, almost certainly derailing it. Congress also has acknowledged its limitations in other fields, especially scientific ones. Most of the time, politicians are wise enough not to intrude on the turf of medical researchers at NIH or engineers at NASA. When they do, the results are never pretty.

Models in Health Care

The idea of using a panel of experts to make recommendations on health policy also has precedent, both here and abroad. After all, since 1931 the FDA has been evaluating the safety of new drugs before allowing them into the marketplace, and since 1962 a manufacturer with a new drug has had to demonstrate to the FDA that its product actually works. Since 1972, various federal agencies have been charged with studying the efficacy and cost-effectiveness of health technologies and treatments. And in beginning in 1987, the U.S. Public Health Service has established task forces to gather evidence on preventive services and create practice guidelines for physicians.

States that have embarked on health-care reform in recent years also have gone one step further to create quasi-independent agencies to make crucial decisions about benefits, standards, and subsidies. In Massachusetts, the Common-wealth Health Insurance Connector Authority is charged with determining which benefits insurance companies must provide. It also decides how much financial help low-income people should get so they can fulfill the state's mandate to purchase insurance. It bears mentioning that the Connector played a crucial political role during the state's health-care debate: Former Governor Mitt Romney, a Republican, and the Democrat-dominated legislature were able to sidestep the potentially poisonous benefits issue by agreeing to let the Connector settle it after the bill became law. Indeed, the Connector continues to actively guide policy in Massachusetts, to help implement this first-in-the-nation plan. And in Maine, the Maine Quality Forum collects research, promotes best practices, and helps residents of that state choose the best doctors and hospitals.

But unlike other industrialized countries, the United States doesn't have a single entity tasked with recommending treatment and coverage policies nationwide. The Agency for Health-Care Research and Quality, the Veterans Affairs hospital system, the Blue Cross/Blue Shield Association, the American College of Physicians, the American College of Cardiology, and the American College of Obstetrics and Gynecology are among the numerous public and private entities that produce reports on new treatments and procedures, but the impact of their research depends on whether employers and insurers use it to make coverage decisions. The National Association of Insurance Commissioners suggests standards for health insurance, but these standards have not lessened the wide variation in practice. This decentralized approach is especially striking in the Medicare program, which has a dual system for deciding what the government will cover. Under Medicare, national coverage decisions are made by the Centers for Medicare and Medicaid Service (CMS). But CMS, which doesn't weigh cost-effectiveness, only hands down about two dozen decisions a year. The remaining 90 percent of Medicare coverage decisions are issued by roughly fifty fiscal intermediaries and insurance carriers scattered around the country.[5] In a 2006 study comparing the U.S. system to that of Great Britain, the author concluded that:

> The United States avoided coming to terms with escalating health care costs and possibly diminishing returns on investments in health care. Perhaps more than anyone else, Americans value technological progress in medical care. The national bias in favor of innovation, along with the dispersion of responsibility for coverage decisions in American health care, makes it particularly difficult to focus public attention on the consequences of our "default" approach to allocating health care resources.[6]

Furthermore, in this country the manufacturers of new drugs and devices can wield significant influence over whether

Medicare covers their products, and how much the government will reimburse hospitals for them. The story of a high-tech technique for spotting breast cancer in mammograms is one example. In 1998, the FDA approved computer-aided detection, which was supposed to improve the interpretation of mammograms by flagging suspicious areas on the breast X-ray for the radiologist to review. The agency approved the new technology based on early reports that it uncovered about 20 percent more cases of breast cancer than mammograms viewed by humans. The manufacturers of the technology also lobbied Congress, which increased the reimbursement rate for computer-aided detection, boosting sales of the machines. But a study published recently in the *New England Journal of Medicine* found that the technology detects suspicious lumps that are not cancer, leading to unnecessary biopsies. Another example: In 2003, the Bush administration ran up against the power of the health-care lobby when it proposed cutting the Medicare payments for some complex treatments and new technologies by as much as 30 percent. The goal, according to then-HHS Secretary Tommy Thompson, was to revamp a payment system that encouraged hospitals to provide "treatments that happen to be the most profitable." But the White House had to back down after the health-care industry complained to members of Congress, wrote dozens of letters to the Medicare agency, and ran advertisements decrying the move.

Forty years ago, the practice of medicine was far simpler than it is today. With fewer tools at their disposal, individual doctors didn't need much outside guidance to help them select the best course of treatment for their patients, and insurers paid for whatever was provided. But as new drugs, surgeries, and diagnostic tools have been introduced, medicine has become more complex. Undoubtedly, many of these advances have led to dramatically improved outcomes for patients. Thanks to new drugs, treatments, and procedures, the overall mortality rate from heart attacks fell by almost half between 1980 and 2000, from 345 to 186 per 100,000 people.[7] Thirty years ago, a diagnosis of testicular cancer was a death sentence. Today, 96 percent of those diagnosed with the disease survive with the help of chemotherapy.[8]

In many cases, however, U.S. doctors employ new procedures or use expensive high-tech equipment even when there is little scientific evidence that the benefits to the patient will be worth the costs. Some analysts believe that up to 30 percent of the care we receive today is unnecessary. Many patients with insurance want any care that might do some good, and plenty of doctors will oblige them. Sometimes doctors do things they don't believe are medically necessary because they want to defend themselves against lawsuits.

More troubling is the idea that some doctors order tests, perform procedures, and prescribe drugs because they have a financial stake in doing so. A recent *New York Times* analysis of records in Minnesota, the only state where drug company marketing payments to doctors are made public, strongly suggests that psychiatrists in that state who received money from drug manufacturers prescribed their products more often. Between 2000 and 2005, the newspaper found, drug company payments to Minnesota psychiatrists rose more than sixfold, to $1.6 million. During the same period, prescriptions of antipsychotics for children in Medicaid increased more than ninefold. The doctors who got the most money prescribed the drugs most often.[9] The same week, *The New York Times* ran a story revealing that Amgen and Johnson & Johnson had been paying hundreds of millions of dollars to doctors every year in return for prescribing anemia drugs which might be unsafe. In a recently released report, the U.S. Food and Drug Administration found no evidence that the drugs improve quality of life in patients or extend their survival, and suggested that they might even shorten lives when used at high doses. The drugs are the single biggest pharmaceutical expense for Medicare, and are given to about a million patients each year to treat anemia caused by kidney disease or cancer chemotherapy. American dialysis patients get doses that are twice as high as what European patients typically get, and cancer patients in the United States are about three times as likely to get the drug as their European counterparts.[10]

Catching diseases before they worsen can save both lives and money. But there is evidence that American doctors are overusing expensive diagnostic equipment and performing procedures that aren't necessary. A recent study on the use of angioplasties, a procedure in which the doctor restores blood flow to the heart by inflating a tiny balloon in an artery narrowed by a blood clot, illustrates the point. Angioplasties can save the lives of people who are in the midst of a heart attack, but they have dubious value to patients who aren't in imminent danger of dying. The researchers looked at 828 angioplasties done on Medicare beneficiaries and found that only a third of the patients could have been expected to benefit from the procedure. In 14 percent of the cases, the angioplasties were completely inappropriate, and in the remaining half it was impossible to determine whether the patients stood to benefit.

The authors of the study concluded that the rising popularity of angiograms, the imaging test that shows narrowing of the arteries, was to blame. When the test revealed a narrowing of the artery, however slight, cardiologists couldn't resist doing something about it, even if urging the patient to exercise more and eat better would have made more sense. Health-care journalist Shannon Brownlee has noted that an annual checkup for a middle-aged man or woman now includes a battery of diagnostic tests that didn't exist two decades ago. Some of these tests have proven their worth as tools for detecting diseases before symptoms appear. Others, however, "are having the perverse effect of benefiting only a small minority of patients while exposing the majority to invasive, often risky treatment they don't necessarily need."

> First, doctors discover that a procedure saves lives or effectively treats an acute condition. Next they begin applying it to patients whose disease is not so advanced in the hope that they will keep the condition from worsening. And then they begin looking for earlier and earlier signs of the disease in patients who feel perfectly healthy. Prevention has become the doctor's watchword, the mantra that drives the use—and often misuse—of procedures and diagnostic tests in every branch of medicine from cardiology to psychiatry. Its pursuit has blurred the boundaries of medical futility and helped fuel the conviction shared by doctors and patients that it is better to err on the side of doing more rather than less.[11]

In many American communities, hospitals are engaged in a technology arms race, competing to attract aging baby boomers with the latest diagnostic imaging machines. PET and CT scans can help doctors estimate the spread of cancer or the extent of cardiac disease without surgery or other invasive procedures. But according to National Imaging Associates, a New Jersey firm that handles radiological benefits for health plans in thirty states, about a third of the advanced imaging tests that doctors order are unnecessary. PET scanners can cost up to $3 million each to install, but they are a good investment because they bring in high payments from Medicare and private insurers. A single scan can cost as much as $3,000. Medicare has pumped up demand by increasing the number of approved uses for the machines: Between 2000 and 2005, it expanded the number of diagnostic tests for cancer that require PET scanners from three to twenty-three. Medicare spending on all imaging services nearly doubled between 1999 and 2003, to a whopping $12 billion. In 1990, Americans got 1.8 million MRI scans and 13.3 million CT scans. By 2003, the numbers had risen to 24.2 million and 50.1 million.[12]

Stanford economist Victor R. Fuchs has pointed out that new technologies in health care aren't bound by the same cost-benefit constraints that prevail in other industries. When auto makers develop a new, more fuel-efficient engine, for example, they know that buyers will weigh fuel savings against the higher cost of the engine. The manufacturer won't produce the engine if the savings don't exceed the costs.

Many investigators believe that even though the total value of health care is large relative to expenditures, a significant portion of spending is for health services of limited or zero value. This can occur for several reasons. Physicians and hospital administrators don't know what the benefits are because the information may not exist or may not have been adequately communicated. Fear of malpractice suits may induce interventions of limited value. Probably most important, financial incentives may be misaligned. Fully insured patients will want any care that might do them some good, regardless of cost. Physicians may feel obliged to provide that level of care.[13]

Another problem is that many doctors find it impossible to keep up with the latest findings. In a landmark 2001 study on the quality of care in the United States, the Institute of Medicine concluded that our health-care system "frequently falls short in its ability to translate knowledge into practice, and to apply new technologies safely and appropriately."[14] The study noted that it takes an average of seventeen years for new knowledge from clinical trials to be put into practice, and that even then it tends to be applied unevenly.

Health care harms patients too frequently and routinely fails to deliver its potential benefits. Indeed, between the health care that we now have and the health care we could have lies not just a gap, but a chasm. Medical science and technology have advanced at an unprecedented rate during the past half-century. In tandem has come growing complexity of health care, which today is characterized by more to know, more to do, more to manage, more to watch, and more people involved than ever before. Faced with such rapid changes, the nation's health care delivery

system has fallen far short in its ability to translate knowledge into practice and to apply new technology safely and
appropriately. And if the system cannot consistently deliver today's science and technology, it is even less prepared to respond to the extraordinary advances that surely
will emerge during the coming decades.[15]

In other countries, national health boards have helped ensure
quality and rein in costs in the face of these challenges. In Great
Britain, for example, the National Institute for Health and Clinical Excellence (NICE), which is part of the National Health
Service (NHS), is the single entity responsible for providing
guidance on the use of new and existing drugs, treatments,
and procedures. Health-care providers, patients, caregivers, and
members of the general public suggest topics for the agency,
which makes its decisions based on clinical research and the expertise of royal medical colleges, professional organizations, and
advocacy groups. NICE also weighs what it calls "economic evidence," or how well the medicine or treatment works in relation
to how much it costs.

In assessing new health technologies, including drugs, the
agency's Centre for Health Technology Evaluation relies on an
independent committee comprised of health professionals and
people familiar with the concerns of patients and caregivers.
The panel reviews the clinical evidence and seeks comment
from doctors, patients, caregivers, manufacturers, and government officials. NICE conducts thirty to fifty appraisals each
year. If the agency determines that a new technology is cost-
effective, NHS authorities in England and Wales must make it
available within three months. NICE's Centre for Clinical

Practice issues advice on the best treatment and care of people with specific diseases and conditions. In addition to guiding physicians, its recommendations are used to evaluate individual doctors and to train them. The Centre for Public Health Excellence focuses on prevention, seeking to promote healthy habits among all citizens. Once NICE issues guidelines and disseminates them, doctors and hospitals are expected to take them "fully into account when deciding which treatments to give people."[16] Doctors are expected to be familiar with the NICE recommendations, but ultimately it is up to them to decide how to treat their patients.

In Germany, the Federal Joint Committee performs many of the same functions that NICE does in Great Britain. The main body of the Joint Committee is comprised of nine representatives from the German "sickness funds" (the roughly three hundred publicly financed health plans that people making less than a certain income must join, and that many earning more money voluntarily join) and nine representatives of doctor, dentist, and hospital groups. There are two neutral members— one proposed by each side—and a neutral chairperson agreed to by both sides. The Joint Committee is responsible for assessing new technologies, determining which drugs, treatments, and procedures will be covered by the state, and issuing directives on proper treatment.

The Federal Ministry of Health reviews all of the Joint Committee's decisions. If the ministry doesn't object within two months, the Committee's directives become binding for all health plans, providers, and patients. When the Committee decides to include a certain technology in the state's benefit catalogue, a separate Valuation Committee, comprised of providers and representatives of the sickness funds, determines the relative value of the new technology compared to existing ones. Germany also has an Institute for Quality and Efficiency, a quasi-independent agency financed by stakeholders rather than the government. The institute is responsible for evaluating the safety and efficacy of drugs, writing scientific reports on the quality and efficiency of health benefits, issuing guidelines on treating certain diseases, compiling up-to-date research on how to diagnose and treat certain diseases, and providing the public with information on the quality and efficiency of care.[17]

In Switzerland, which has a public-private health-care system that many Americans might find appealing, any medical service that is added to the basic benefits package that all Swiss insurers must offer has to meet standards of clinical effectiveness, appropriateness, and cost-effectiveness. In that country, the Federal Social Insurance Office regulates private insurers to make sure they are offering coverage to anyone who wants it, and are charging everyone in a given area the same premium. All Swiss citizens are required to purchase at least the basic package of benefits, which is comparable to a comprehensive policy in the United States or Germany.

Structure and History
of the Federal Reserve System

The Federal Health Board I envision for our country would be modeled on the U.S. Federal Reserve System, which has skillfully managed monetary policy for decades while earning a reputation for political independence. Created in 1913, the Federal Reserve aims to maintain low interest rates while promoting economic expansion. Its primary tool is open market operations, that is, the purchase or sale of securities to affect the money supply. It also has a broad range of supervisory and regulatory responsibilities for the banking industry. It is financed through its own activities, and returns its profits to the U.S. Treasury. Significantly, it requires no appropriation from Congress. The "Fed," as it is popularly known, has three levels. The first is a Board of Governors, composed of seven members appointed by the president and approved by the Senate. The Board members have staggered fourteen-year terms, with a chairman and vice chairman appointed by the president for four-year terms. Generally, Board members are nominated to serve based on their expertise in economics and monetary policy. Second, there are twelve regional Federal Reserve Banks, managed by their own nine-member boards of directors. In addition to partial representation in the open market operations, the regional Federal Reserve Banks carry out the daily operations of the system, including its general supervisory authority. The third tier of the Fed is its member banks—all banks chartered by the Federal government, and state-chartered banks. About 40 percent of all federally insured U.S. banks are member banks. The entire system is supported by about five hundred career staff, the majority of whom are analysts or economists.

To understand what makes the Federal Reserve System successful, it's helpful to consider how it evolved over time.

Congress wanted it to be an independent entity so it could formulate the nation's monetary policy without being influenced by political and private pressures. It is no accident that it was born during the Progressive Era, when reformers wanted to make government more objective and less political. But when lawmakers gave the Fed the authority to coin money and "regulate the value thereof," they had only a vague idea of what they wanted the bank to accomplish, other than to prevent the bank runs and panics of the past. The original structure of the Fed reflected a compromise among competing concerns. It had a centralized body, the Board of Governors, to appease large East Coast bankers, and a dozen regional banks to assuage the fears of small bankers and farmers scattered around the country. But by 1930, the Fed was floundering. Its mission was too vague, and the reserve banks were acting independently of the Board of Governors. The Fed had effectively become an arm of the Treasury, which forced it to hold down interest rates on the bonds it issued, which resulted in inflation.

The Banking Act of 1935 revised the structure of the Fed into its current form, solidifying the power of the Board of Governors and creating the new role of chairman. That solved the problem of the rebellious regional banks, but it didn't free the Fed from the control of the Treasury. During World War II, the Treasury sought to finance the war by selling low-interest bonds, and the Fed reluctantly agreed to peg interest rates to the Treasury's desires, despite its concerns about inflation. An informal agreement in 1951 between the Treasury and the Fed, known as "the Accord," freed the Fed from its obligation to support the Treasury's low interest rates. For the first time, the Fed was truly independent, and during the next two decades it matured into a powerful economic force.

The most recent evolutionary phase in the history of the Fed occurred in the 1970s, when simultaneous high interest rates and high unemployment—previously thought to be economically impossible—incurred the anger of Congress. In response, lawmakers beefed up their oversight of the Fed by instituting reporting, hearing, and auditing requirements. Former Fed chairman Alan Greenspan highlighted the importance of this transparency in a 1996 speech. His arguments are just as relevant to the health board I am proposing.

> If we are to maintain the confidence of the American people, it is vitally important that, excepting the certain areas where the premature release of information could frustrate our legislated mission, the Fed must be as transparent as any agency of government. It cannot be acceptable in a democratic society that a group of unelected individuals are vested with important responsibilities, without being open to full public scrutiny and accountability.[18]

Fed Board members are recognized experts, and they set policy based on data and analysis. Few members of Congress are trained economists. Their lack of expertise, compounded by the daily political pressures they face, would prevent them from making sound decisions in such a complicated arena. Many politicians recognize this: Political scientist Donald F. Kettl has pointed out that for the most part, Congress and the

White House have been happy to leave monetary decisions to the Fed, especially when the action that is economically prudent promises short-term pain.

> The final point is that elected officials have shown little taste for taking direct responsibility for monetary policy. The Fed has the discretion it enjoys because Congress chooses to allow (indeed, to encourage) it. The benefits of this discretion to members of Congress have been clearly demonstrated in the [Former Chairman Paul] Volcker era. They could allow the Fed to take the painful steps that the anti-inflation campaign required, bemoan the awful results of tight money, escape the even more awful political implications of trying to balance the federal budget, and in the end achieve lower inflation and improved economic growth. President Reagan and his staff, meanwhile, could tacitly support the Fed's wrenching policies without having to embrace them publicly.[19]

The Fed is largely insulated from the politics and passions of the moment, but it would be a mistake to assume that Congress and the White House have relinquished all control over monetary policy. First, members of the Board of Governors are political appointees, chosen by the president and confirmed by the Senate. Second, the Fed derives its authority from Congress, and Congress can dismantle it whenever it wants. Third, elected politicians have laid out the Fed's mission: to pursue both "maximum employment" and "stable prices." The Fed isn't free to ignore, amend, or supplement those directives. Finally, Congress has the power to overturn a Fed decision or remove a governor for good cause, though it has never done either.

According to Kettl, the independence of the Fed "is only a precondition for power, not power itself. The Fed's power depends on the support it can build, not on its legal status. Without political support, its credibility is low, its effectiveness is sharply limited, and its legal independence is fragile."[20]

In the same 1996 speech, Greenspan argued that if Congress or the president micromanaged the Fed, "short-term political forces would soon dominate. The clear political preference for lower interest rates would unleash inflationary forces, inflicting severe damage on our economy." At the same time, Greenspan emphasized that the Fed is ultimately accountable to the American people:

> This process is not easy to get right at all times, and it is often difficult to convey to the American people, whose support is essential to our mission. Because the Fed is perceived as being capable of significantly affecting the lives of all Americans, that we should be subject to constant scrutiny should not come as any surprise. Indeed, speaking as a citizen, and not Fed Chairman, I would be concerned were it otherwise. Our monetary policy independence is conditional on pursuing policies that are broadly acceptable to the American people and their representatives in the Congress.[21]

Even though the Fed has to answer to the public, it is sufficiently insulated, so that its decision-making process hardly resembles what goes in Congress or the White House. In Congress, every decision is political. It's impossible to formulate policy without weighing the likely reactions of special interests, the other party, influential committee chairs, and the president. The next election is always just around the corner, so it's hard to get lawmakers to think in the long term. The Fed, in contrast, can make decisions based on data and a thorough analysis of what's best for the country. The effects of monetary policy take a long time to manifest themselves in the economy, and sometimes it is necessary to suffer through short-term pain to advance the long-term goal of keeping inflation in check. It's hard to imagine that lawmakers up for re-election would be able to resist the short-term benefits of lower interest rates. Alan Blinder, who served on President Clinton's Council of Economic Advisers and was a member of the Board of Governors, has a unique perspective on the different environments:

> Regardless of who is president, life at the White House is fast-paced, exhilarating, and—of necessity—highly political. Policy discussions may begin with the merits ("Which option is best for the American public?"), but the debate quickly turns to such cosmic questions as whether the chair of the relevant congressional subcommittee would support the policy, which interest groups would be for or against it, what the "message" would be, and how that message would play in Peoria . . . at the Federal Reserve, on the other hand, the pace is deliberate, sometimes plodding. Policy discussions are serious, even somber, and disagreements are almost always over a policy's economic, social, or legal merits, not its political marketability. Overtly partisan talk is deemed not just inappropriate, but ill-mannered. The attitudes of particular legislators, interest groups, or political parties toward monetary policy are rarely mentioned, for they are considered irrelevant. And the Fed rarely discusses its "message."[22]

There is a strong argument to be made that appointed experts, proceeding in a "deliberate, sometimes plodding" way, would make better health-care decisions than politicians. Like monetary policy, health-care policy shouldn't be subject to the whims of subcommittee chairmen and special interests. It is too complicated and too important for that. As new drugs, treatments, and procedures continue to proliferate, and the financial stakes rise higher and higher, it will be increasingly difficult for politicians to make the right health-care choices. After nearly a century of failure, it's time to try another way. That is why I believe we should create a "Federal Health Board" that has the knowledge to make complicated medical decisions and the independence to resist political pressures. During the push for reform, the promise of a board would allow legislators to defer some of the tough technical decisions that have derailed previous efforts. And once a bill was passed, the board could help define evidence-based health benefits and lower overall spending by determining which medicines, treatments, and procedures are most effective—and identifying those that do not justify their high price tags. It also could play a vital regulatory role, ensuring that accurate information on providers, insurers, and purchasing pools is made available to the public. The health board also would emulate some of the regulatory functions of the Securities Exchange Commission. Like the SEC, it would ensure that the public has accurate information on providers and health plans. Broadly speaking, the board would oversee the health-care industry in the same way that the SEC oversees securities exchanges, brokers, and dealers. It might, for example, regulate the marketing of drugs to doctors and consumers. In part four, I will explore this idea in greater detail.

Part Four

THE FEDERAL HEALTH BOARD

If our nation is headed for another dramatic debate over health care—and I believe it is—what should we be aiming for? What should a reformed health-care system look like? We will wrangle over the route, but I think most of us can agree on the destination: a seamless, value-oriented system that offers affordable health care to everyone. Whatever plan we come up with, it must expand access, lower costs, and improve quality. Making sure that everybody has insurance is essential. If we don't reach that goal, it will be difficult to control costs and improve quality. If every American is covered, however, we can align our payments and policies to promote best practices and encourage efficiency.

A Federal Health Board would have both political and practical benefits. It would help us break the legislative logjam that has blocked previous attempts at comprehensive reform, and it would establish a strong public framework for a high-performing, private health system. At the end of this chapter, I will describe the board in detail, but first I'd like to sketch out a broader vision of how the U.S. health-care system should and could function in the near future.

Framework for the
U.S. Health-Care System

MOST PEOPLE AGREE that a reformed system must focus on access, affordability, and quality. To achieve this, it must ensure that all Americans not only can enter the coverage system but are protected once in. The system should strive to get the best possible outcome for each health-care dollar spent. It should strengthen the backbone of the system—its infrastructure—to even out the delivery and efficiency of care. And it should promote shared responsibility: We must take collective and individual responsibility for the health of the nation. Each of these five elements of a strong health system is described below.

Options for Coverage

The key question for any health-care reform plan is, "How will it cover people?" Most of the world's highest-ranking health-care systems employ some kind of a "single-payer" strategy—that is, the government, directly or through insurers, is responsible for paying doctors, hospitals, and other health-care providers. Supporters say single-payer is brilliantly simple, ensures equity by providing all people with the same benefits, and saves billions of dollars by creating economies of scale and streamlining administration. But a pure single-payer system is politically problematic in the United States, at least right now. Even though polls show that seniors are happier with Medicare than younger people are with their private insurance, opponents of reform have demonized government-run systems as "socialized medicine." The health-care industry fears that government-set reimbursement will limit its ability to provide care and deaden incentives to develop new drugs and cures. Furthermore, many people who have insurance now are satisfied with it, and are wary of change.

If passage of a single-payer system isn't realistic, what should we do? Conservatives tout the idea of liberating individuals from employers and groups and allowing them to shop for insurance on their own. The rationale is that there is no one-size-fits-all insurance, and that market-based forces coupled with consumerism can solve our system problems. I am dubious of these claims, based on the evidence and my own experience. High-cost sharing leads to reduced use of both needed and unneeded care. Employers are increasingly rejecting it as a successful way to contain costs. And people enrolled in these plans may be gaining cost consciousness—but are also becoming angry voters. They do not like high premiums followed by high deductibles followed by high co-payments.

Another alternative is to strengthen our current employer-based health-care system. In the United States, most people with health insurance get it through their employers. If your employer helps pay your premiums, or can offer you insurance at a group rate, you are likely to have coverage. Some argue that employers should be obligated to offer health benefits to their workers. Supporters of an "employer mandate" say it would result in coverage for nearly everyone, since 80 percent of the uninsured are attached to the workforce. But we should be wary of creating a system that relies exclusively on employers. What about people who lose their jobs, or leave the workforce temporarily to take care of small children or elderly parents? What about those who are self-employed, or work part-time? The job-insurance link can create a vicious cycle: If you don't have insurance you are less likely to visit a doctor, which might make your health problems worse, which might make it more difficult for you to work. Sometimes, the process works in reverse: Health problems lead to employment problems, which leads to a loss of coverage, which leads to worse health problems.

So instead of creating a "pure model" system, I believe we should build on the one that we have. Nearly 80 percent of Americans are covered through the employer-based system, Medicaid, the State Children's Health Insurance Program, and Medicare. We should maintain and strengthen these kinds of coverage. But to reach everybody else, I believe that we should expand the Federal Employee Health Benefits Program (FEHBP), or create a group purchasing pool like it.

FEHBP is a menu of private health plans that is offered exclusively to federal employees and members of Congress, covering more than eight million workers and their dependents. I know from personal experience that this is an excellent system. Why not open it up to everybody without job-based insurance? Employers and their employees might prefer greater choices of affordable plans in the new national pool and should be allowed to join.

Under the system I envision, meaningful choices would be maintained. Participants could choose their own providers and would have the security of knowing they could never lose their coverage. Nobody would be barred from obtaining health care outside the FEHBP, just as people who want to forgo the public school system and pay extra to send their children to a private school are free to do so. The crucial point is that the FEHBP plans would guarantee a basic set of benefits to everybody.

One of the options under the expanded FEHBP should be a government-run insurance program modeled after Medicare, a proven and popular program. Together with traditional Medicare, this new program would have tremendous clout to bargain for the lowest prices from providers and push them to improve the quality of care. It also could take advantage of the administrative efficiencies, further lowering costs. (Medicare's administrative costs are significantly lower than those in the private sector.)

Because some people wouldn't be able to afford insurance, even the least expensive policies on the FEHBP menu, the government would provide financial help on a sliding scale to those in need. Perhaps we could guarantee that nobody has to pay more than a certain percentage of their income for health insurance. This protection, administered as a refundable tax credit, would apply to employer-based health insurance as well as private insurance obtained through the pool.

Employers with successful health programs could retain them; if the tax incentives for offering health benefits remain in place, it is reasonable to assume that many would stand pat. But small businesses straining under the weight of rising premiums might prefer to let their employees get coverage through a FEHBP plan. However, employers could participate only if they enrolled all of their workers, not just ones with health problems.

In addition to creating a FEHBP-like system, we must strengthen Medicaid. This program has become a pillar of our insurance system, recently surpassing Medicare in its enrollment. It now serves about 50 million of the nation's most vulnerable children, low-income parents, people with disabilities, and seniors. Yet eligibility varies from state to state, and major gaps in the program exist. Most notably, Medicaid does not cover poor adults who are childless and don't have disabilities.

The story of Monique "Nikki" White, a young woman from Bristol, Tennessee, illustrates why solidifying Medicaid is so essential. When she was twenty-one, in 1994, Monique was diagnosed with lupus, a disease in which the immune system attacks healthy tissue. Though lupus can be fatal and there is no cure, there is medication to keep it under control. Monique was covered by her parents' insurance until 1999, when she left college. After leaving school, she worked at a Barnes & Noble bookstore and then at a hospital trauma unit in Austin, Texas, which provided health benefits. But in 2001 her lupus worsened, and she had to quit her job in Texas and move into a garage apartment next to her parents' house in Bristol. Because of her condition, no private insurer would sell her a policy at any cost. Tennessee had expanded its Medicaid program, Tenn-Care, in 1994, to cover uninsured adults and people with pre-existing conditions, and Monique's mother begged her to apply. Monique didn't want to be on welfare, but finally she relented and joined the program in October 2003. She began seeing a doctor regularly.

When Monique's condition worsened in early 2005, her doctor referred her to a local rheumatologist, one of the few in the area willing to accept TennCare patients. The rheumatologist prescribed a drug to treat her symptoms, and ordered a follow-up CT scan, blood tests, and frequent return visits. He wanted to keep close tabs on her because both lupus and the drug he had prescribed can damage the liver, blood, and pancreas. But Monique never went back: During the summer Tenn-Care eliminated her coverage. The program had grown to cover nearly a quarter of Tennessee's population, and the state tightened eligibility requirements to save money. Monique appealed the decision. In the meantime, she went for months without medical care because she couldn't afford it. As a result, her health deteriorated.

In November 2005, Monique had a seizure and had to be rushed to Wellmont Bristol Regional Medical Center. Doctors there found that her kidneys had failed, her liver was failing, and her intestines were perforated. In the next ten weeks, doctors at Bristol Regional performed more than two dozen operations to clean up recurring dead tissue. The nonprofit hospital absorbed the $900,000 cost of her care, and she seemed to be recovering.

In February, however, doctors found a fungal growth near her heart valve. Bristol Regional wasn't equipped to perform the necessary surgery, so Monique was transferred to Duke University Medical Center in Durham, North Carolina. On May 28, two weeks after she suffered a stroke, her heart stopped.

About a week later, Tennessee sent a letter to Monique notifying her that it had put her back on the Medicaid rolls.

"She'd probably have stayed [alive] if she had TennCare," Monique's doctor, Dr. Amylyn Crawford, told *The Wall Street Journal.* "No one can say that it caused the problems. [But] it did have an impact on her, on her stress level, and on her access to medical care, particularly specialty care."[1]

This heartbreaking story is an eloquent argument for simplifying and extending Medicaid to cover everyone below a certain income level, perhaps up to 150 percent of the federal poverty level. The federal government should pick up the tab for this expansion, and ensure that states don't cut off people like Monique White when the budget gets tight.

What "Coverage" Means

A reformed system built upon an expanded FEHBP, employers, and Medicaid and Medicare would cover everyone. But what kind of coverage would it be? Today, many insured Americans who become ill or are injured discover that their policies don't cover the care they need, or cover so little they are forced to run up huge medical bills. Health insurance should truly insure Americans against costs that block access to needed care or induce financial distress.

As well as covering high costs, a reformed health system should be aggressive in promoting prevention. Unfortunately, our system gives short shrift to prevention programs and low-tech methods that can be as effective, or more effective, than high-tech interventions. In his book *Your Money or Your Life: Strong Medicine for America's Health Care System*, David Cutler cites the care of premature babies as an example. In the last several decades we've developed high-tech equipment and procedures that have dramatically improved the survival rate of babies with low birth weights. But this care comes with a high price tag, often costing more than $100,000. In contrast, we do relatively little to promote a strategy that would be just as effective and much cheaper: convincing expectant mothers to quit smoking. Smokers are twice as likely to have low-birth-weight babies. Giving them advice on how to quit, paying for cessation aids, and following up with them regularly would cost about $50 per woman.[2]

Another glaring omission from our health coverage system is mental health care. In recent decades we've come a long way in our understanding and treatment of mental illness, and the stigma associated with it has dissipated. Nevertheless, both public and private insurance plans still place restrictions on mental health coverage that don't exist for other health problems. If a good friend of mine had had his way, there would be no such disparity. The late Senator Paul Wellstone of Minnesota, who watched his brother suffer from mental illness, made mental health–care coverage a passion during his tenure in the Senate. He introduced a bill in 1992 with Pete Domenici of New Mexico, whose daughter had struggled with mental illness, to prohibit insurers from setting annual or lifetime dollar limits on treatment for mental illness. The bill was signed into law in 1996, but almost immediately insurers took advantage of unintended loopholes to avoid the requirement that they treat mental health on par with physical health. Undeterred, Paul introduced a new bill. More times than I can remember, he stood on the Senate floor, blocking action on any other legislation until we acted on his commonsense proposal to prohibit group health plans from imposing unfair restrictions on mental health coverage. Since Paul's death, his sons have taken up his crusade on mental health parity, pushing Congress to end limits on days or treatment visits and exorbitant co-payments or deductibles.

In reforming our health-care system, we should fulfill Paul's vision by promoting parity in the coverage of mental and physical ailments. In Medicare, for example, there is a lifetime limit of 190 days for inpatient psychiatric treatment, even though there is no corresponding limit on general hospital care. Medicare generally covers 80 percent of the cost of outpatient care for physical ailments, but only 50 percent of the cost of outpatient care for mental illnesses. This may be remedied in Congress in 2007, but even doing so is not enough. Private plans also tend to treat mental and physical illnesses differently. In 1996, Congress sought to address this issue by mandating limited parity in insurance provided by businesses with fifty or more workers. But the law does not prevent companies from setting higher deductibles or co-payments for mental health benefits, or from doing away with mental health coverage altogether. Despite the federal law, and parity laws in thirty-three states, gaps persist. People with mental health coverage through their employers often face limits on how many times they can visit an outpatient provider, as well as on the number of days they can receive inpatient care.[3] In contrast, Medicaid offers mental health coverage without many of the restrictions of Medicare and private plans, as well as critical services such as respite care and case management. It doesn't exclude people with pre-existing conditions, or impose a waiting period. In tight fiscal times, however, states are often tempted to cut back on Medicaid mental health benefits, which are costly. We should shore up the program with federal dollars so mental health doesn't get short shrift during trying economic times.

In 2002, a presidential panel convened to study the state of mental health services in the United States concluded that "for too many Americans with mental illnesses, the mental health services and supports they need remain fragmented, disconnected, and often inadequate."

> State-of-the-art treatments, based on decades of research, are not being transferred from research to community settings. In many communities, access to quality care is poor, resulting in wasted resources and lost opportunities for recovery. More individuals could recover from even the most serious mental illnesses if they had access in their communities to treatment and supports that are tailored to their needs . . . in short, the nation must replace unnecessary institutional care with efficient, effective community services that people can count on. It needs to integrate programs that are fragmented across levels of government and among many agencies.[4]

Long-term care is another area we must address. Our over-sixty-five population will grow from 36 million in 2000 to 78 million in 2040, according to the U.S. Census Bureau. More people are remaining active at an advanced age, but longer life expectancies almost certainly will increase the need for long-term care. Medicaid covers long-term care, but only for low-income families. And Medicare only pays for care that is connected to a hospital discharge. I believe that our health-care system must cover these vital services, either through Medicare or by making long-term care coverage a requirement for FEHBP participation. Furthermore, we should promote home-based care, which most people prefer, instead of the institutional care that we emphasize now.

A reformed health-care system also should guarantee that every American has access to affordable dental care. Not surprisingly, people with dental insurance are more likely to visit the dentist regularly for preventive care that those without it. Even when a serious problem develops, many uninsured people avoid getting dental treatment because they simply can't afford it. The tragic story of twelve-year-old Deamonte Driver of Maryland illustrates the dangers of this approach. Tooth decay is the most common childhood disease in the United States—five times as common as asthma. Poor children are more than twice as likely to have cavities as those from more affluent families, but they are far less likely to get treatment. The Driver family didn't have steady health insurance—the boy's mother worked in a series of bakery, construction, and home health-care jobs that didn't provide it—and Deamonte and his siblings never got routine dental care, although they qualified for Medicaid coverage. One day in January 2007, Deamonte came home from school complaining of a headache. At a local hospital emergency room, he was given medicine for a headache, sinusitis, and a dental abscess. But the next day he felt even worse; the bacteria from the abscess had spread to his brain. Eventually, he was rushed to another hospital, where doctors performed emergency brain surgery. After he began to have seizures, they operated again, and the problem tooth was extracted. For weeks it looked as though Deamonte would recover, but at the end of February, he succumbed to the infection.[5]

The Driver family's Medicaid coverage had lapsed at the time Deamonte was hospitalized. But even if it hadn't, it isn't clear he would have gotten the dental care he so desperately needed. That's because Medicaid reimbursement rates are so low that in many areas relatively few dentists will accept Medicaid patients. In a congressional hearing held in the wake of Deamonte's death, a dentist and dental-care advocate from Prince George's County, where the boy lived, testified that for families on Medicaid, "it is virtually impossible for a parent to find a dentist to treat their child's dental concerns." Dr. Frederick Clark said there are only two hundred dental offices listed as providers for the roughly 50,000 Prince George's children enrolled in Medicaid. When Clark and his aides contacted the dentists to confirm their participation, only a fourth of them said they would see a child on Medicaid.[6]

Sered and Fernandopulle point out that for adults, a lack of dental care also can have economic consequences. The two researchers tell the story of Loretta, a Mississippi woman married to a self-employed contractor: Loretta's five children were covered by Medicaid, but she and her husband were not, and they couldn't afford to purchase insurance on their own. When Sered and Fernandopulle visited Loretta in her home, they were struck by the fact that she was missing almost all of her teeth. "I've gotten toothaches so bad, so that I literally pull my own teeth. They'll break off after a while, and then you just grab ahold of them, and they work their way out," Loretta told them. "It hurts so bad, because the tooth aches. Then it's a relief just to get it out of there. The hole closes up itself anyway, so it's so much better."[7] The researchers argue that Loretta's appearance almost certainly harms her employment prospects:

> Her physical appearance (missing and rotten teeth, a near-sighted squint, and her generally unkempt presentation) makes it unlikely that she can fulfill her dream of a job in a veterinarian's office, where she would be dealing with the public. She is more likely to be steered toward jobs like the one she found shortly before we met her—conducting a phone survey during the evening hours at the local university. In other words, Loretta is bright enough to participate in a university research project, but she is not considered presentable enough to work in an office where she would meet clients or research subjects face-to-face. Loretta's work at the university is temporary, part-time, and dead-end. Because she's a "temp," the university does not provide health insurance.[8]

Increase Value

So far, I have outlined how we should cover everybody, and the types of services that coverage should include. But in reforming the system, we also have to cut costs and improve quality. Covering everybody will move us forward in both of these areas. After all, people without insurance receive sporadic, low-quality care, and when they are treated in emergency rooms and can't pay their bills, the cost of their care is passed on to the rest of us. Doctors and hospitals charge higher fees to recoup their losses. Insurers, in turn, raise premiums and deductibles. Some analysts estimate that each uninsured person costs the average insured family about $900 a year.

To make more significant progress, however, we have to concentrate more on the *value* of the care we are getting. We can and should strive to get more for our health-care money by steering providers toward drugs, treatments, and procedures that yield the best results at the lowest cost. We should spend money on expensive new technologies that benefit patients, but we shouldn't waste it on ineffective, poor-quality care. The Institute of Medicine highlighted the value, or the lack thereof, in our health-care system in a report released in 2001:

> The health care system as currently structured does not, as a whole, make the best use of its resources. There is little doubt that the aging population and increased patient demand for new services, technologies and drugs are contributing to the steady increase in health care expenditures, but so, too, is waste. Many types of medical errors result in the subsequent need for additional health care services to treat patients who have been harmed. A highly fragmented delivery system that largely lacks even rudimentary clinical

information capabilities results in poorly designed care processes characterized by unnecessary duplication of services and long waiting times and delays.[9]

Today, most health research focuses on whether a particular medicine or treatment is safe and works. We should go further by promoting research that *compares* drugs and treatments to determine which ones deliver the best bang for the buck. Does an over-the-counter drug work as well as a brand-name prescription drug? What are the relative merits of heart disease treatment options? These are the kinds of questions we should be asking. The answers would help patients, providers, and payers make more sensible health-care choices. We also should sponsor more research on how new technologies—the main driver of rising health-care costs—should be deployed. Many new tests and procedures, while valuable for some patients, are overused. Research that identifies the kinds of patients who might benefit from a new technology would help control costs in the long term.

Clearly, choosing the right medical procedure is not the same as buying the right television. But if we want to get health-care costs under control, we're going to have to pay more attention to whether we are getting our money's worth. Milton Weinstein, a professor of medicine at Harvard University who has examined this issue, argues that the United States lags far behind other nations in this regard.

One question that is rarely asked, at least in polite company, is whether we're getting the most health improvement possible for our money. In other words, are all the things that we do in medicine really worth it? That is where cost-effectiveness comes in. As a nation, we have been unwilling, at least publicly, to look explicitly at value, in terms of improved health outcome, that we get for our health care dollars. With advances in medical technology putting unsustainable pressure on health care costs, our historical reluctance to measure value for health care may have to change.[10]

Through Medicaid, Medicare, and its other health programs, the federal government is responsible for a huge proportion of total health-care spending. If the FEHBP is transformed into a national insurance pool, that proportion will grow even larger. The federal government could exert tremendous leverage with its decisions on covered benefits and payment incentives. In choosing what it will cover and how much it will pay, it could steer providers to the services that are the most clinically valuable and cost-effective, and dissuade them from wasting time and money on those that are neither. As we saw in the last chapter, other nations are forging ahead of us in this area.

The federal government also should measure the quality of providers, and make the results public. Patients and their families should have information that allows them to choose the best hospital, health plan, doctor, or treatment. In crafting standards for care, federal programs should pay particular attention to the diseases and conditions that affect the most Americans: cancer, diabetes, emphysema, high cholesterol, HIV/AIDS, hypertension, heart disease, stroke, arthritis, asthma, gallbladder disease, stomach ulcers, back problems, Alzheimer's and other dementias, and depression. In our fragmented health-care system, only the federal government is in a position to develop national quality standards that everyone would follow—and it would cost relatively little for it to do so. In Great Britain, the National Institute on Clinical Excellence (NICE), which develops guidelines for the National Health Service (NHS), spends less than 1 percent a year of its total national health spending.

One way Washington could spark improvement would be to tie payment to performance, instead of basing it solely on the services delivered. In its 2001 report, the Institute of Medicine concluded that "the current health-care environment is replete with examples of payment policies that work against the efforts of clinicians, health-care administrators, and others to improve quality."[11] Currently, third-party payment for medical services is based on the value the third party places on services, as well as what providers are willing to accept. The value that patients place on a service never enters the equation. Doctors and hospitals that provide better services don't get paid a higher rate, even though some patients might be willing to pay more for higher-quality care. A shift to pay-for-performance in federal programs would alter this dynamic, and likely would spill over into the private sector.

We also could lower costs by focusing more of our energies on prevention. Our current system focuses too much on treating diseases, and not enough on keeping people healthy. And with no guarantee that enrollees will remain in their plans, insurers have little incentive to invest in keeping them healthy over time. In addition to ensuring coverage of prevention, we should dedicate funding and attention to public health efforts. Doing so could improve our nation's overall health and yield substantial savings. For example, studies suggest that a staggering 27 percent of the growth in health-care costs between 1987 and 2001 was connected to the rising incidence of obesity during that period. This trend cannot be reversed with a drug or surgery: Exercise and nutrition changes are necessary, and best implemented in communities, schools, and the workplace.

A reformed health-care system also should place a greater emphasis on treating chronic conditions, rather than focusing so intently on acute care. Chronic conditions are now the leading cause of illness, disability, and death in the United States, and nearly half of the American people have one or more of them. As a nation, we now spend most of our health-care dollars on chronic care, but we still have a health-care system that is geared toward providing acute care. Care for people who are chronically ill has to be collaborative, since it often involves multiple providers. Communication between patients, doctors, and caregivers is crucial, and health information has to follow patients as they move from home to doctor's office to hospital to nursing home and back. And yet too often, doctors and hospitals in our country operate in isolation, providing care without having complete information about a patient's condition, medical history, or previous care they might have received.[12]

This is especially true of the poor and uninsured. Those

who lack health insurance rarely go to the doctor, so they simply endure their chronic conditions until the pain becomes unbearable or there is an emergency. A 2006 study found that 59 percent of uninsured adults with a chronic condition did not fill a prescription, or skipped their medications, because they could not afford them. And more than one-third of chronically ill adults without insurance went to the emergency room or stayed overnight in the hospital during the previous year because of their condition—twice the rate of adults with insurance.[13] Two researchers, Susan Starr Sered and Rushika Fernandopulle, who traveled the country in 2003 and 2004 interviewing people without insurance reported that coordination of care is a rarity. The researchers interviewed about 120 people without health insurance. Of that number,

> no one reported having a family doctor who knows the medical history of family members, who knows how the patient has responded in the past to particular medicines, who knows the family's risk factors, who has any inkling about the family's ability to follow through on medical instructions, or who is poised to provide any sort of health education, nutrition counseling, or continuity of care. Such a sporadic approach does not serve anyone well. Continuity of care is associated with greater use of preventive services and better control of many chronic illnesses, such as hypertension and diabetes. It also leads to fewer hospitalizations and to lower overall health care costs.[14]

This illustrates how the value of care can only improve when we end the problem of uninsurance.

Infrastructure

With each passing day, the Internet assumes a more significant role in people's daily lives, and yet our supposedly high-tech health-care system is stuck in the information dark ages. Incredibly, only 5 percent of clinicians have computerized patient records and only a small fraction of the billions of medical transactions that take place each year in the United States are conducted electronically. The latest information technology, structured to safeguard patients' privacy, has the potential to dramatically cut costs and improve health-care quality. The ability to consult a patient's full medical history online would make it easier for doctors to deliver the most appropriate care. Public health officials could use the database to detect trends, and to determine the value of different treatments for specific kinds of patients.

A 2005 study attempted to quantify the savings we might glean from a fully electronic, connected health-care system, and they are substantial. Consider laboratories, for example. Many doctors and hospitals rely on external labs. Connecting them electronically would reduce delays and costs associated with paper-based ordering and reporting of results, for a possible savings of as much as $31.8 billion annually. Similarly, many doctors and hospitals send patients to external radiology centers. Connecting them by computer also would save time, and cut costs associated with paper- and film-based processes, saving as much as $26.2 billion annually. Internet transactions between providers and payers might save $20 billion every year. If all doctors were connected by computer, they could save time handling referrals and chart requests, saving as much as $13.2 billion annually. And ensuring electronic communication between doctors and pharmacies would decrease the number of medication-related phone calls and make it easier to prevent duplicate therapy and harmful drug interactions. Possible annual savings: $2.7 billion. Overall, the researchers concluded, a fully electronic health-care system could save us as much as $77.8 billion annually, or approximately 5 percent of the roughly $1.66 trillion we spent on health care in 2003.[15]

Historically, Washington has played a leading role in accelerating the spread of new farming technologies, and it could do much more to drag health-care information systems into the twenty-first century. It could, for example, create tax breaks for health-care providers that adopt the latest information technologies, or offer loans or loan guarantees to health-care institutions—especially nonprofit ones—seeking to upgrade their computer systems. There is precedent for such a step: After 1946, when many hospitals were crumbling after the Depression and World War II, the federal government handed out loans and grants to hospitals on the condition that they provide free or discounted care to people unable to pay for it. The government also could set national standards for clinical computing, and serve as a clearinghouse of information about effective computing practices.[16]

In rural states such as mine, South Dakota, one of the main health-care challenges is a lack of providers. Many rural residents have to spend hours in a car or even get on a plane to get the care they need because the nearest medical specialist is hundreds of miles away. It can be difficult to convince doctors to practice in rural areas, where they earn far less money. We can do more to recruit them, as well as link providers to such communities through technology. Physicians can use interactive video to communicate with patients in a faraway town or state, and in a fully computerized, integrated health-care system it would be possible for local doctors to send pictures, X-rays, and other patient information directly to the computer of a specialist.

Finally, we should increase the number of community health centers, government-funded clinics that provide basic care to the poor and uninsured. These clinics are a godsend for many people across the country, particularly those who live in rural areas with a shortage of health-care providers. Even if we achieve "universal" coverage, there will be some percentage of people who still fall through the cracks. These clinics will serve as a safety net. This is one area where I must applaud President Bush: He has expanded the number of community health centers by nearly a third since he took office. That said, more needs to be done.

Shared Responsibility

The last element of a new framework for American health care is the division of responsibility. In my opinion, every player in the health-care arena—the government, employers, doctors and hospitals, insurers, and individuals—should help support a rational, sustainable system.

The government should shoulder more of the burden. In our country, we have more than 5,500 acute care hospitals,

18,000 nursing homes, and 800,000 doctors. There are licensure boards and regulatory agencies in every state, multiple accrediting organizations, and hundreds of professional organizations, boards, and societies. There are hundreds of insurance companies and health plans, and thousands of employers who self-insure.[17] In a health-care system with so many actors, there is only one with the clout to improve quality and control costs: the federal government. Through Medicare, Medicaid, SCHIP, the Veterans Affairs department, the Pentagon, and the Indian Health Service, the federal government provides health care to roughly 100 million people. But these programs offer different benefits to different people, with no uniform system for measuring outcomes.

If there were a single standard of care and coverage in all of these programs, it would be a model for every other provider and payer. If the federal government computerized all its health records, or insisted on linking pay to performance, there would be tremendous pressure on everybody else to follow suit. If we had a more rational system for gauging the value of tests, treatments, and procedures, we could improve quality and get a handle on health-care costs.

Employers also have a vital role to play. Some already are doing a lot—too much, in fact. As I discussed earlier, companies such as G.M. are spending such huge sums on medical care for current workers, retirees, and their families that they are struggling to compete. Other employers don't do enough, either contributing too little or not at all to their workers' coverage. I believe that the right balance is in between: providing an FEHBP-like group purchasing pool, and assistance independent of work, but allowing employers to either con-tinue to cover workers or help finance the pool's coverage. This would allow employers to choose how to fulfill their re-sponsibility, while ensuring that this responsibility is fairly shared by all employers.

Doctors, hospitals, and other health-care providers will have to adjust to a value-oriented system. In too many cases, they are providing care that doesn't reflect the latest science. That will have to change. They will have to learn to operate less like solo practitioners and more like team members, working with providers in other practices, hospitals, and even states, to coor-dinate care. In return, they will enjoy the benefits of working in a simpler, seamless system that recognizes and rewards excellent performance.

Insurers that want to participate in the FEHBP-like pool will have to follow federal rules on coverage and cost. They likely will be barred from denying coverage to high-risk, high-cost people, and might face limits on the amount of money they can spend on marketing. These new rules will come with rewards: a consistently insured set of enrollees and govern-ment backing to ensure that those who struggle can afford to pay premiums.

Individual Americans also will have new obligations in a re-formed health-care system. The only way we can achieve uni-versal coverage is to require everybody to either purchase private insurance or enroll in a public program. As long as we can make health insurance affordable and accessible for every-one, this is a reasonable requirement. In the plan I envision, the federal government might levy an income-based assessment on those who fail to purchase coverage, ensuring that they contribute to the cost of care they will inevitably use.

The idea of a so-called individual mandate is hardly unprecedented. Parents must make sure their children are vaccinated to enroll them in school, and every driver has to buy auto insurance. Moreover, the landmark universal coverage plan that Massachusetts recently approved includes an individual mandate. Beginning in 2007, residents of that state who cannot prove that they have health insurance will be denied the personal exemption on their state income taxes, which is worth $219 for an individual. The penalties will increase over time. Former Massachusetts Governor Romney called an individual mandate "the ultimate conservative idea, which is that people have responsibility for their own care, and they don't look to government to take care of them if they can afford to take care of themselves."[18] In fact, the individual mandate idea is attracting adherents from across the political spectrum. The need for a mandate is one of the few things that Senator Ted Kennedy and former House Speaker Newt Gingrich agree on. Republican California Governor Arnold Schwarzenegger included it in his own health-care proposal. Other backers include former Clinton Administration HHS Secretary Donna Shalala, former Bush Administration HHS Secretary Tommy Thompson, the Heritage Foundation, and the Center for American Progress.

In a truly successful health-care system, Americans will have to take more responsibility for their own health. Chronic illness and obesity are epidemics with tremendous human and financial costs. The government can use its bully pulpit to promote public health, and employers and schools should be encouraged to sponsor on-site exercise and nutrition programs. But ultimately, it's up to each one of us to take ownership of our own health and well-being.

The Federal Health Board

My vision for the health system is similar to those of others, and hopefully shared by the public at large.[19] But I do not believe we should draft a bill laying out this vision in excruciating detail. Doing so would ignore one of the mistakes of the early 1990s, when President Clinton submitted his bill to Congress as a finished product. It also locks into place a plan that seems reasonable today but may be outdated tomorrow, given rapid changes in health care.

I believe a Federal Health Board should be charged with establishing the system's framework and filling in most of the details. This independent board would be insulated from political pressure and, at the same time, accountable to elected officials and the American people. This would make it capable of making the complex decisions inherent in promoting health system performance. It also would give it the flexibility to make tough changes that have eluded Congress in the past.

Structure

The Federal Health Board would be a quasi-governmental organization. It would have a board of governors consisting of clinicians, health benefit managers, economists, researchers, and other respected experts. Governors would be chosen based on their stature, knowledge, and experience, ensuring that the decisions they make have credibility across the health-care spectrum. The president would appoint them to Senate-confirmed, ten-year terms. The value of long terms is that they span any single president, ensure continuity and expertise, and limit the potential conflicts of interest that come from the "revolving door" of people coming in and out of public service.

The Federal Health Board also would have regional boards that would have a say in national decisions, but would focus primarily on promoting best practices and quality of care locally. While the national board would be comprised of experts, the regional boards would include community and business representatives with no conflicts of interest. They would concentrate on fulfilling national priorities, and identifying the best local practices and propagating them. Over time, the regional boards might assume other roles, such as ensuring an adequate supply of certain services or linking payment to performance. The regional board would help anchor the national board in the "real world" of the health delivery system.

Like the Federal Reserve Board, the Federal Health Board would have a staff of analysts charged with assessing and producing the research required to make sound decisions.

These analysts would include insurance underwriters, nurse-researchers, economists, engineers, scientists, and policy experts, among others. Because of the importance of the Federal Health Board's recommendations, the staff reports and information would be both rigorous and transparent. In an ideal world, the staff would have access to privacy-protected electronic health record data to use to identify what works and what doesn't. The Board and its staff would have unparalleled resources, and would produce work that would become part of the public domain.

Functions

Congress will have the final say on the Board's powers, but I envision it performing several crucial functions. First, it would set the rules for the expanded FEHBP, placing conditions on the private insurers wishing to participate. It might, for example, develop guidelines on premiums and marketing practices. It would implement policies to prevent insurers from shunning high-cost enrollees. In overseeing the pool, the Board would aim to promote competition, curb administrative costs, and protect consumers. The Federal Health Board also would work with Medicare to develop a public insurance option for the pool, designing it to compete with the private insurance plans on the FEHBP menu. The Board's guidance would aim to maintain choice in insurance, reduce the administrative costs, promote good insurer practices, and protect consumers.

Second, the Federal Health Board would promote "high-value" medical care by recommending coverage of those drugs and procedures backed by solid evidence. It would exert influence by ranking services and therapies by their health and cost impacts. In addition to conducting its own research, the Board would suggest research priorities for the National Institutes of Health and other agencies, and analyze all other federal health data, including the electronic health records from the Veterans Administration and Medicare. It would make its decisions in public meetings, with mandatory reports to Congress.

In some areas, the Board's work would be easy. Promoting prevention, for example, is relatively simple and painless—even Congress could do it. It is not so clean-cut to determine which back pain or mental illness treatment is the most clinically valuable and cost effective. We won't be able to make a significant dent in health-care spending without getting into the nitty-gritty of which treatments are the most clinically valuable and cost effective. That means taking a harder look at the real costs and benefits of new drugs and procedures. In Great Britain, NICE, described in part three, uses cost-effectiveness information in deciding whether to cover a new drug or procedure. I'm not suggesting that we should adopt a hard-and-fast rule on cost-effectiveness in public policy. Nevertheless, it is clear that as a nation we have to begin to look at medical care in a different way. The challenge, as David Mechanic of Rutgers University points out, is creating an entity with the credibility and the clout to make those tough decisions. Mechanic agrees that a board modeled on the Federal Reserve might be the answer.

Important to the evidence-based effort is building credible ways to evaluate the quality of the research, study biases, and applicability of research to patients different from those studied in randomized controlled trials and other studies. Such credible evaluators can offer the best informed consensus on the state of current knowledge. Many public and private organizations are attempting to do this, but it is necessary for them to collaborate on a strategy and speak with fewer and more credible voices. An independent organization with impeccable scientific credentials, and with public participation could play a central role, perhaps using the UK's NICE as a model. The organization might be structured along the lines of the Federal Reserve, working closely with government but more insulated from everyday politics than typical government agencies.[20]

Promoting value in health care is not just about quality: it could reduce costs. In a January 2007 survey, health-care opinion leaders (a group that included health-care providers, professors, insurers, drug manufacturers, and government officials) said that using evidence-based guidelines and cutting down on inappropriate care were the most effective ways to control rising health-care costs.[21] Peter Orszag, who heads the Congressional Budget Office, recently said that creating a research hub where analysts would determine which treatments work best would result in a "significant reduction in health-care costs, including Medicare and Medicaid costs."[22] We all pay more when patients receive the wrong treatments and fail to recover as quickly as they could. We also pay more when doctors employ new procedures or use expensive high-tech equipment when the patient would be better off with a low-tech alternative—or no care at all. The Federal Health Board might be the research hub that experts envision. The regional boards of the new system could facilitate the adoption of best practices identified through this process.

In his 2002 book, *Complications: A Surgeon's Notes on an Imperfect Science*, surgeon and *New Yorker* staff writer Atul Gawande discusses the treatment of patients known to have had heart attacks. Studies have proven that aspirin alone can save lives, and that even more people can be saved if doctors immediately use a thrombolytic, a clot-dissolving drug. And yet doctors only give aspirin to three-quarters of the patients who should get it, and they administer a thrombolytic to only half of the people who would benefit from it. In some parts of the country, doctors comply with evidence-based guidelines more than 80 percent of the time, but in others, the percentage is as low as 20 percent.[23] Local collaboration, consistent standards, and adequate support through a Federal Health Board would be a vehicle for spreading the latest evidence-based guidelines around the country.

A third function of the Federal Health Board would be to align incentives with high-quality care. Through direct-to-consumer advertising, drug companies have ramped up patient demand for some new drugs that are no better than older, cheaper alternatives. They also have spent millions wooing doctors, plying them with fancy dinners and rewarding them with bonuses when they prescribe their products. In describing the first American College of Surgeons convention he attended, Gawande offers a glimpse into this world. Held in a huge convention hall in Chicago, the gathering was "as much trade show as teaching conference," according to the young surgeon.

> Ads for cool new things you had never heard of—a tissue-stapling device that staples without staples, a fiber-optic scope that lets you see in three dimensions—ran night and day on my hotel room television and even on the shuttle bus to and from the convention center. Drug and medical device companies offered invitations to free dinners around town nightly. And there were over five thousand three hundred salespeople from some twelve hundred companies registered in attendance here—more than one for every two surgeons.[24]

Gawande also recalls joining a crowd of about fifty surgeons clustered around a projection screen showing live video of a patient undergoing the excision of an internal hemorrhoid in an operating room in Pennsylvania. The manufacturer of a new device sponsored the show to prove that the product could help shorten the procedure from a half hour to less than five minutes. "Then he put the device before the camera. It was white and shiny and lovely. Against any high-minded desire to stick to hard evidence about whether the technology was actually useful, effective, and reliable, we were all transfixed.[25] Under my plan, the Federal Health Board would counter the smoke and mirrors with hard facts on the value of devices, drugs, and services.

The Federal Health Board can also help create the right incentives by paying providers based on health outcomes, rather than on services delivered. There is evidence that doing so would both improve health and lower costs. In the late 1990s, for example, a Minneapolis health plan decided to create a bonus system for doctors treating patients with diabetes. HealthPartners, a nonprofit with 630,000 members, paid doctors extra if their diabetic patients got their blood sugar and cholesterol below certain levels, quit smoking, and took aspirin daily. In 1996, only 5 percent of the patients met all the criteria, but by 2003 the percentage had risen to 17 percent. HealthPartners achieved similar results with heart patients. In 2003, the plan awarded $9 million in bonuses, or about $330 per patient. But an economic analysis of the program determined that HealthPartners could expect to save roughly $30,000 over each patient's life.[26]

In the last several years, Medicare has been experimenting with different incentives, including rewarding doctors for keeping costs down. Most experts predict that if Medicare adopts pay-for-performance there will be tremendous pressure on private health plans to follow suit. In addition to awarding bonuses for better outcomes, Medicare could pay more for operations that are recommended, and less for procedures and drugs that seem discretionary. In his 2004 book *Your Money or Your Life: Strong Medicine for America's Health Care System*, David Cutler writes that, "Ultimately, the medical system works the way the incentives steer it. Rather than fight the system or plead for it to be otherwise, we should instead line the incentive up right so the system gives us what we want."

Suppose that Medicare and private insurers paid physicians more when depressed patients were appropriately treated than when they were not, and that private insurers earned additional income from having a lower burden of depression among their enrollees. This would create financial incentives for providers to work toward effective treatment of the mentally ill. People would be encouraged to come in at the appropriate times and would be given the right medications. Dropping out of therapy would be reduced. No longer would pharmaceutical companies' incentives be the only ones encouraging more use.[27]

In addition to paying providers based on their performance and their adherence to evidence-based guidelines, the Federal Health Board could promote quality and save money by making the health-care system more transparent. Today, there is so much cost shifting in our system, it is virtually impossible for people to grasp what they are paying for, or to find out which providers and treatments get the best results for the least amount of money. Health economist Uwe Reinhardt has compared the U.S. health market to an imaginary world in which employers agree to reimburse their workers for 80 percent of the "reasonable cost" of clothes deemed "necessary" and "appropriate" for the office, but the employees have to shop blindfolded. Then, months after the shopping trip, a fiscal intermediary sends an "Explanation of Benefits" to the employee telling him or her how much to pay.[28]

Because prices and success rates are shrouded in secrecy, there can be an alarming disconnect between cost and quality in our health-care system. In June 2007, Pennsylvania's Health Care Cost Containment Council released the results of a survey of the state's sixty hospitals that perform heart-bypass surgery. The agency found that the cost of the surgery was as little as $20,000 at one hospital and nearly $100,000 at another. And yet at both hospitals, patients had comparable lengths of stay and death rates. Furthermore, two of the highest-paid hospitals in metropolitan Philadelphia had abnormally high death rates. "It doesn't make sense," said Marc P. Volavka, who heads the Health Care Cost Containment Council. "Certain payers are paying an awful lot for poor quality."[29]

The lack of transparency in the health-care system hides problems and makes it difficult for patients, providers, and payers to recognize and reward high-value care. It's nearly impossible for patients to find the performance records of doctors and hospitals or to compare their costs. Providers often have no clue about the prices of the procedures and treatments they recommend to patients. Employers, the government, and other payers often sign blank checks to doctors and hospitals, unable or unwilling to determine whether they will be charged a fair price.

Finally, the Federal Health Board also might play a role in rationalizing our health-care infrastructure. Because of its fragmentation, the U.S. health system lacks a "map" to guide its resource investments. We have too many imaging machines in some areas, and too few emergency rooms in others. Furthermore, we have no mechanism that enables us to direct resources to certain areas when a desperate need arises, whether it is a spike in infant mortality rates in Mississippi, or a jump in the number of people with diabetes on an Indian reservation. As the entity tasked with closing the gap between the ideal health-care system and the flawed reality, the Federal Health Board might issue an annual report on what investments are needed where. Hopefully, these recommendations would be heeded by federal, state, and local officials, as well as private organizations interested in making a difference.

Enforcement

The Federal Health Board wouldn't be a regulatory agency, but its recommendations would have teeth because all federal health programs would have to abide by them, and those programs account for 32 percent of all health spending and insure roughly 100 million Americans. Making one set of policies for all federally funded health programs is common sense.

In the past, private insurers have followed Medicare's lead in areas such as refining the hospital payment system, and the Board's coverage decisions could have the same spillover effect. Private insurers participating in the new FEHBP might find it hard to maintain separate sets of rules for enrollees inside and outside the pool, and employers might use the Board's recommendations as a guide in crafting their own health benefits packages. Furthermore, Congress could opt to go further with the Board's recommendations. It could, for example, link the tax exclusion for health insurance to insurance that complies with the Board's recommendations. That said, the goal is a Board that is a standard setter that allows a private delivery system to operate within a public framework. A highly regulatory approach is unlikely to succeed.

Conclusion

The idea of a Federal Health Board is only one part of the solution to our nation's health-care crisis. Any comprehensive reform plan must provide affordable coverage to all Americans, and to do so responsibility must be shared. For example, Congress would need to create a framework for financing health coverage, and the executive branch would have to implement key elements of the reform plan, such as promoting the information technology infrastructure we so sorely lack. We'll be able to wrest power from Congress and the White House only when political leaders realize that they are incapable of making the technical decisions on benefits that are so crucial in any health-care system. I believe that this time is coming. A Federal Health Board could be the key that finally unlocks the door to high-quality, high-value health care.

Part Five

PROSPECTS FOR HEALTH REFORM

Health care is back at the top of the national agenda. Once again, it is a dinner-table topic for millions of American families, and a looming presence in an intensifying presidential campaign. In many ways, the current climate reminds me of 1991. That year, Harris Wofford's upset victory in Pennsylvania seemed to signal that, after decades of failure, the time for reform had finally arrived. Then, as now, the excitement was palpable, and optimism was high.

Are we on the verge of enacting health reform, or is this déjà vu all over again? Is public support strong enough to tolerate the inevitable disruptions that real change will bring? Are interest groups interested only in pain-free reform? Will we make the same mistakes we made in the past? In this chapter, I explore the prospects for reform and explain why I think that the Federal Health Board may be the answer to solving this puzzle.

Drumbeat for Health Reform

As our current crisis deepens, it is getting harder to ignore the potential benefits of comprehensive reform. First and foremost, universal coverage would help millions of Americans live longer, more productive lives. As I noted in part 1, the Institute of Medicine has estimated that a lack of health insurance leads to 18,000 unnecessary deaths each year. Many people who are uninsured or underinsured forgo preventive care, delay treatment for their medical conditions, or skimp on drugs. When a serious illness is permitted to progress, a patient is less likely to survive and care is more expensive. If everyone had insurance, hospitals wouldn't be under pressure to recoup the costs of caring for the uninsured by raising fees on everybody else. Universal coverage also would give a boost to the economy by reducing the number of sick days and improving workers' productivity. Health-care reform that effectively controls costs would put more money in Americans' pocketbooks, both by reducing what they spend on medical care and by making it possible for employers to raise their wages. It would provide relief to businesses straining under the burden of fast-rising premiums, and it would give a much-needed boost to companies struggling to compete in the global marketplace. A more transparent health-care system, with a sharper focus on quality control, would empower patients to choose the best providers and treatments. There would be fewer medical errors, and a greater emphasis on the chronic conditions that plague the most Americans.

Interest in reform may be even more intense now than it was in the early 1990s. In numerous polls, Americans have pointed to health care as the nation's second most pressing problem, after the war in Iraq. A whopping 70 percent of the participants in a *New York Times*/CBS News poll in February 2007 described the large number of uninsured people as a "very serious" problem. Sixty-four percent said the federal government should guarantee health insurance to all Americans, and 60 percent said they'd be willing to pay higher taxes to achieve that goal. A poll by the same news organizations, conducted in July 1994 during our last health-care debate, found that only 55 percent of respondents were willing to pay higher taxes to cover everybody. The same 2007 *New York Times*/CBS News poll found that 59 percent of Americans were "very dissatisfied" with the cost of health care in the United States, and another 22 percent were "somewhat dissatisfied." In addition, the survey uncovered anxiety about future costs, with 52 percent of respondents saying they were "very concerned" about what they might have to pay in the future. Every major Democratic candidate in the 2008 presidential field—and a few of the Republicans—have pledged to expand health-care coverage and lower costs. In the absence of federal action, states from Massachusetts to California are tackling the problem themselves.

I see a lot in the current landscape that bodes well for reform. In the early 1990s, a recession and widespread job insecurity drove the debate forward. To a large extent, the discussion then revolved around job loss and low-income people without insurance. Today, health care is a concern for a wider swath of the population, because rising health-care costs are affecting everyone, even those who have health insurance. Almost 85 percent of Americans have health insurance, so the problem of the uninsured affects them only indirectly. The health-care problem that is burdening the most people, the one that can rally individual Americans and powerful interest groups to the cause of reform, is cost. People are paying higher premiums, higher deductibles, and higher co-payments, and they are rightfully anxious about it.

A survey conducted by the Employee Benefit Research Institute in the fall of 2006 is illustrative. In the group's ninth annual Health Confidence Survey, 52 percent of participants said they were "not too satisfied" or "not at all satisfied" with the cost of health insurance—the highest percentage in the history of the poll. Sixty percent of the respondents said they experienced a rise in the last year in the amount they had to pay for their insurance, and 55 percent said reining in costs should be the top health-care priority for Congress, while only 38 percent named improved access to health care.

We should remember that the main reason there are more Americans without insurance is that the cost of health care is rising so rapidly. As costs have exploded, more employers have dropped or scaled back coverage for their workers, and individuals looking to buy insurance on the private market have had a harder time finding plans they can afford. Many states have scaled back their Medicaid programs, cutting people from the rolls to save money. Many states and cities are struggling to cover their own employees.

Cost is also the main concern of a constituency that could make or break the reform effort: business. Despite the recent decline in employer-sponsored coverage, employers still provide health benefits to about 60 percent of the U.S. population, and they have been struggling to pay health premiums that have increased 98 percent between 2000 and 2007, compared with an overall inflation rate of about 23 percent during that period.[1] The skyrocketing costs are making it difficult for many U.S. companies to compete against their international rivals, most of whom don't have health-care expenses. In part 1, I noted that Ford and GM pay nearly $1,500 in health-care costs for each vehicle they produce, while BMW pays $450 per vehicle in Germany, and Honda $150 per vehicle in Japan. By 2008, General Motors fears its health-care costs could add $2,000 to the sticker price of every car it makes. Rising health expenses weigh heavily on U.S. businesses as they decide how to price their products, whether to hire more workers, and how much to invest in research and development. Many workers don't realize it, but high health costs also lower their wages.

It seems that every few weeks another group of businesses bands together to push for reform. In February of 2007, the Center for American Progress helped form a coalition dedicated to achieving comprehensive health reform by 2012. Its leading members are Wal-Mart and the Service Employees International Union (SEIU). In May 2007, three dozen Fortune 500 companies, including Safeway, Pepsi, General Mills, Kraft, CVS, and Kaiser Permanente, launched a coalition that backs a market-based approach to universal coverage by 2009. In June 2007, the Business Roundtable, an association of CEOs whose companies employ more than 10 million people, partnered with AARP and SEIU to form Divided We Fail. It, too, embraces affordable coverage for all. The group noted that "our members consistently name health-care costs as the number-one cost pressure facing them in their leadership of America's largest companies."

> Rising health care costs are affecting America's workers, consumers, employers and government; inhibiting job creation; and hurting our ability to compete in global markets. Health care costs are straining the household incomes of many Americans, leaving them without insurance and adequate health care. Congress must address the issue of the uninsured.[2]

Most surprising to me are recent statements by the National Federation of Independent Business (NFIB), which represents small business owners. NFIB was one of the most vigorous opponents of President Clinton's health-care plan in the early 1990s. During that debate, NFIB pressured key lawmakers by sending mass mailings to their constituents, and it held seminars around the country to highlight how the Clinton plan would harm local businesspeople. The group also ran a masterful media campaign that fueled the public's fear of change. But small businesses are being hit especially hard by rising premiums. In May 2007, NFIB's president and CEO, Todd Stottlemyer, said, "As our country continues to thrive on the jobs created by our entrepreneurs, it is time Congress takes action to address this mounting problem that will inevitably diminish this growth if it continues to go unaddressed." In May 2007, an NFIB poll of its members found that 74 percent of them considered costs to be the most serious issue facing the health-care system.

Another new phenomenon that might help us finally enact reform is the growing power of the Internet and the resulting democratization of the media. Reformers will be able to use blogs, online videos, and other new media tools to counter the big-money ads of special interests, catalyze the public's anger, and turn up the pressure on politicians. Virtual rallies, the twenty-first century's answer to the mass marches of the 1960s, might attract millions of Americans who wouldn't otherwise get involved in the debate.

Finally, the 2008 presidential campaign has been unique in recent history. For the first time in about sixty years, there was no incumbent in the race. No candidate had a legacy to uphold, or was tied to the previous administration's policy failures. As the Bush administration staggered to its conclusion, the American public was hungry for effective leadership and new ideas. An astounding 70 percent of Americans believed we were on the wrong track.

The 2008 presidential candidates were paying attention. Barack Obama, Hillary Clinton, and John Edwards, among the contenders, all proposed ambitious health-care plans that focused on cutting costs, and they shared many of the same ideas for doing so. All three called for a greater emphasis on prevention, computerized record-keeping, better-coordinated care of people with chronic conditions, insurance purchasing pools, and some kind of independent entity to promote comparative research and disseminate the results to providers, insurers, and patients. While Republican primary contenders offered less-detailed and ambitious plans, the public support was bipartisan. In the February 2007 *New York Times*/CBS News poll, 64 percent of Republicans said the U.S. health-care system needs "fundamental changes," and 44 percent of GOP participants said they were "very dissatisfied" with the cost of health care in the country. Another 24 percent of Republicans said they were "somewhat dissatisfied" with high health costs. As such, the 2008 election promised to be a referendum, in part, on a commitment to reforming the health system.

And, behind the scenes, the broad outlines of a reform plan that could win bipartisan support are starting to take shape. First, most people acknowledge that a reform plan must build on existing public and private structures to fill in coverage gaps. This includes a purchasing pool like FEHBP for quality, affordable group health insurance. Employers should retain some responsibility for covering their workers. There also is growing support for the idea that everybody should be required to have some kind of health coverage, a so-called individual mandate. The idea of shared responsibility resonates with conservatives and with progressives alike, as long as insurance is made affordable through subsidies. In Massachusetts, the idea that individuals, businesses, and the government share the responsibility for covering everybody greatly enhanced the plan's political prospects. Most important, there is growing support for the idea that we can cut costs and improve quality by embracing an evidence-based approach to health care. We simply must do a better job of gathering and disseminating the latest research and directing providers to the services that are the most clinically valuable and cost effective. This is the arena in which the Federal Health Board I am proposing can play a vital role.

Perennial Challenges

BUT A GENERAL desire to overhaul the system isn't the same as getting it done. I am a veteran of the battle in the early 1990s, and a student of failed efforts in earlier decades. The current indicators are promising, but they hardly guarantee that we are on the cusp of reform. To succeed, we will have to overcome serious, perennial challenges.

First, health care is incredibly complex. Everybody needs medical care, but few people know much about it. Getting health care isn't like buying a car: The average person is ill-equipped to determine which procedures are necessary and which are wasteful. Furthermore, over the years we have constructed a health delivery system that is positively Byzantine. A South Dakotan in Medicare can expect far different benefits and payments than a South Dakotan enrolled in the Indian Health Service, or one who gets health care from the Veterans Health Administration. When a topic is as complicated as health care, it is relatively easy to misinform the public and stoke fears, no matter how strong the desire for reform.

Second, special interests are especially numerous and influential in the health-care arena. Health care comprises one-sixth of our economy, and the savings we seek will come out of executive's salaries and companies' profits. In terms of political clout, the health-care industry is second to none. Between 1998 and 2006, pharmaceutical companies and other manufacturers of health-care products spent over a billion dollars on lobbying, more than anybody else and twice as much as the oil and gas industries. Insurance companies, including health insurers, ranked second. Since cutting costs is tantamount to cutting profits for many of these special interests, it is reasonable to expect them to engage in all-out war to defeat reform.

To finally succeed, we also will have to overcome powerful and persistent myths about our current health-care system. First and foremost is the mistaken belief that we have the best health care in the world. Imagine what would happen to the head of the U.S. Olympic Committee if we finished thirty-seventh in the medal count during next summer's Olympics. And yet that's where we rank in life expectancy. In some of our communities, people fare even worse. On the Pine Ridge Indian Reservation in South Dakota, for example, the life expectancy is a paltry forty-seven years. We have a system that can't even provide coverage to the men and women who have put their lives on the line for our country: A recent study by a Harvard Medical School professor concluded that about 12.7 percent of nonelderly veterans—about 1.8 million people—lacked health coverage in 2004.[3]

Another myth is that we can't afford to reform the system. Cynics suggest that even the most modest reform proposals will eventually lead to more far-reaching and "encroaching" solutions. But the truth is that we can't afford the status quo. We spend more than $6,400 per American on medical care—more than twice the industrial world's average—and yet we are the only advanced country that fails to cover everyone. Medical bills are the leading cause of bankruptcy in the United States, and a fifth of working-age Americans—with and without insurance—have medical debt they are paying off over time.[4] The question isn't whether we can afford reform, it's how much longer we can afford the current mess.

Unfortunately, these myths are ripe for exploitation. Sometimes, special interests wield them to protect a status quo that is highly profitable to them. In other cases, they are used to advance political goals: Bill Kristol and Newt Gingrich used them to sink President Clinton's health-care reform, paving the way for sweeping GOP victories in the 1994 elections. Beginning in the summer of 2007, I watched in disbelief as President Bush tried to torpedo a bipartisan compromise on the State Children's Health Insurance Program, hoping to deny the Democratic Congress a significant accomplishment as his own administration continues to sink. In so doing, the White House trotted out the same old lines about "government-run health care" and "socialized medicine." The language could have been lifted from the antireform pamphlets of the 1940s.

Cutting the Gordian Knot

ONE KEY TO overcoming these challenges in the coming battle is leadership. During my time in Congress, I was privileged to work with men and women whose vision and political skill improved the lives of millions. But overhauling a healthcare system that represents 16 percent of our economy and affects each and every one of us will require inspired leadership from the White House.

If the next president is dedicated to reform, he or she can use the formidable power of the White House to create a sense of urgency on this issue and forge a consensus on how to move forward. This means going on the offensive; we cannot wait for the next "Harry and Louise" ad to define the debate. We cannot assume that the public recognizes the distortions and fallacies peddled by reform opponents; we have to educate people on the emptiness of antireform rhetoric. The next president should act immediately to capitalize on the goodwill that greets any incoming administration. If that means attaching a health-care plan to the federal budget, so be it. This issue is too important to be stalled by Senate protocol.

And we shouldn't shy away from making the moral argument for change. It is simply unconscionable that in a nation as wealthy and powerful as ours, citizens are forced to go without medical care that could relieve their suffering and extend their lives. Len Nichols, a health-care policy expert at the New America Foundation in Washington, D.C., makes an eloquent case for injecting morality into the debate:

> There are 10,000 technical issues involved with health system reform, but one fundamentally moral question: who shall be allowed to sit at our health care table of plenty? Many scriptural traditions and much humanistic philosophy admonish all communities to feed the hungry. Food was once the only indispensable commodity, the only thing one human being could give to another to guarantee and sustain life, the reason for communities in the first place. Health care has long since joined food as a unique gift, necessary to sustain and enrich lives stricken with certain kinds of illness. . . . For us to deny health insurance—or access to effective health care—because of cost is tantamount to denying food to the starving poor. Few ethical teachers would approve. We can do far, far better than that.[5]

In Massachusetts, a coalition of religious leaders, the Greater Boston Interfaith Coalition, used moral persuasion to become an influential force in the state's health-care debate, playing a key role in the eventual passage of a reform plan. "Every human being is created in the image of God. And if it's so, then every human body is a sacred vessel," Rabbi Jonah

Pesner of Temple Israel in Boston proclaimed at one prore-form event at the Massachusetts state house: "Together we will create a coalition of compassion, and we will do what we know to be right, to be just, to be merciful: to bring health-care access and affordability to each and every member of the Commonwealth."[6] Polls suggest that moral arguments might sway Americans in other states, too. In May 2007, the Pew Re-search Center reported that support for government pro-grams to help disadvantaged Americans, as well as sympathy for the plight of the poor, have surged since 1994, reaching levels not seen since the 1980s. A survey by the center found that 54 percent of Americans believe the government should help more needy people, even if doing so increases the na-tional debt.[7]

We must stay focused on pragmatic solutions, such as the Federal Health Board, and reject rigid ideology. We simply can't let the perfect be the enemy of the good. My three de-cades on Capitol Hill taught me that nearly every piece of leg-islation will harm the interests of at least some people. The challenge is to craft a bill that creates more winners than los-ers, that mitigates the potentially negative effects on the los-ers, and that benefits society as a whole.

I believe that the Federal Health Board meets that standard. If its promotion of evidence-based medicine curbs health-care costs, people who have insurance now would pay less for it. Businesses, both large and small, would get financial relief, as would state and local governments. Insurers might welcome the arrival of an independent entity with the credibility to deny coverage of unproven or ineffective treatments and procedures.

And average Americans would gain the security that comes with stable, quality coverage.

But there would be losers, too. If coverage decisions are taken out of the hands of elected officials, advocacy groups with political clout wouldn't be able to exercise it. Doctors and patients might resent any encroachment on their ability to choose certain treatments, even if they are expensive or ineffective compared to the alternatives. Some insurers might object to new rules that restrict their coverage decisions. And the health-care industry would have to reconsider its business model. Today, investment depends on whether a particular medicine or treatment is safe and works. Requiring proof that a drug or treatment works better than an existing alternative would raise that standard. This would cause some developers of new drugs, devices, and procedures to spend more time and money proving their products' worth, which I believe is good policy as well as good business.

I suspect that most members of Congress would be glad to be rid of their responsibility for controversial health policy decisions. If the Federal Health Board fulfills its mission, it will have to reduce or deny payment for new drugs and procedures that aren't as effective as current ones. Doing so will rankle powerful interest groups, such as drug manufacturers. Who will benefit? Ordinary Americans, a diffuse and unorganized group that isn't likely to reward lawmakers for their complicated coverage decisions. In this respect, the Federal Health Board will be similar to the Federal Aviation Administration (FAA). Congress delegated responsibility for airline safety to the FAA, knowing full well that it would get little credit when planes landed safely, and intense scrutiny when one of them crashed. If the FAA does its job well, the beneficiaries are air travelers, another unorganized group that doesn't have much political clout. In contrast, those who have to bear the costs of regulation, the airline companies, are well organized and politically active. In their 1999 book on the separation of powers, David Epstein and Sharyn O'Halloran of Columbia University argue that "policy will be made in such a way as to maximize legislators' political goals, which we take to be reelection first and foremost. Legislators will prefer to make policy themselves, as long as the political benefits they derive from doing so outweigh the political cost."[8] In Massachusetts, state lawmakers turned over the hard decisions on benefits to the Commonwealth Health Insurance Connector Authority, a move that made it much easier to come to an agreement on a broad reform plan. I am convinced that a similar strategy would brighten the prospects for reform on the federal level as well.

In creating a Federal Health Board, we also will have to assuage the doubts of people who are simply scared of allowing an unelected board of strangers to make such critical decisions. In discussing support for a Fed-like board, Stuart M. Butler of the Heritage Foundation cites "the fear that a remote panel of faceless individuals will make mechanical decisions and cannot be reasoned with—the worry that lies at the heart of the widespread antipathy to insurance companies and particularly to managed care."[9] When the Federal Reserve Board sets interest rates, it affects people's money. But when the Federal Health Board makes coverage decisions, it will affect people's lives. That is why it is so crucial that the Board be transparent and ultimately accountable to elected officials. The Board should make its decisions in public, and Congress should subject it to strict auditing and reporting requirements. Earlier, I quoted former Federal Reserve Chairman Alan Greenspan's observation that "it cannot be acceptable in a democratic society that a group of unelected individuals are vested with important responsibilities, without being open to full public scrutiny and accountability." We must keep that in mind as we create the guidelines for the Federal Health Board.

Furthermore, we must emphasize the fact that unlike the decision-makers at insurance companies, the members of the Federal Health Board will serve at the pleasure of elected officials. They will be political appointees, chosen by the president and confirmed by the Senate. The board will derive its authority from Congress, and Congress can dismantle it whenever it wants. Congress will have the power to overturn a board decision or remove a board member for good cause, although I hope it will use this power sparingly, if ever. I also stress that the board will only have direct authority over federal programs and private participants in the FEHBP, and won't have regulatory power to impose standards on other private insurers.

The Federal Health Board would serve as a public framework for a private health system. It would make tough coverage decisions, collect evidence, identify weaknesses in our system, and align federal health programs. Hopefully, it would become more than the sum of its functions. Like the Federal Reserve, it could evolve into an institution worthy of trust, a body of experts judged to be immune from political machinations. Will it work? I'm sure the same question was posed when President Roosevelt and Congress created the Federal Reserve nearly a century ago. Today, it is absurd to imagine Congress debating interest rates. Creating a new entity to fulfill that function made sense in 1913; doing the same thing for health care makes sense now.

Conclusion

It isn't hard to make the case for health reform, and the outline of a consensus plan is emerging. Our current system falls short on access, quality, and cost. We can make substantial improvements in all three areas by building on the private-public hybrid we have now. We have 47 million people without insurance, but about 250 million do have coverage. We can expand access to health care by extending public and private group health insurance to all Americans. Medical errors may result in as many as 98,000 deaths a year, but we have some of the best medical minds in our country, and some of the most advanced medical practices. Surely we can improve upon this record. The best medical care costs money, but most experts believe we can significantly reduce our costs without harming the quality of care.

But to enact health reform, we'll have to overcome some significant barriers. On the left, there are still many who insist the United States should sever the link between employers and health insurance and adopt a government-run, single-payer system like those of European countries. But compared to residents of those countries, Americans are more supportive of choice and suspicious of government. Moreover, business groups and conservatives will not support it. Many purists on the right continue to place their faith in Health Savings Accounts and tax credits. But those measures won't significantly reduce the number of uninsured, and they don't offer much help to the sickest Americans. Americans are generally wary of strategies that shift more costs and risks onto them, while doing nothing to get costs under control.[1] A hybrid solution also has its flaws, but it has one distinct advantage over the others: It is politically and practically feasible.

We must remember that this isn't an academic debate. Millions of Americans have suffered, and thousands have died, because our current system is broken. This is all too clear in the story of Michael Loncar. The forty-nine-year-old had a history of lung and liver problems, could not work, and had no health insurance. His wife, who had health problems of her own, had recently gotten insurance through her job at Wal-Mart, but could not afford it for her husband or two children—especially in light of the $40,000 the family owed to a nearby nonprofit hospital where Michael recently had surgery. This all meant that, one morning, when Michael was coughing up fluid, he ignored his wife's urging that he go to the emergency room. He feared racking up new bills, or being asked to pay the old ones. He died while she was at work. The story is not over, since the hospital chased down his widow to garner her wages to pay off the debt.[2] Michael's death certificate listed a health condition, but he and his family are really victims of our failure to fix the system.

I have strong views on what an "ideal" system would look like. But I'm not willing to sacrifice worthy improvements on the altar of perfection. I find it encouraging that the leading Democratic presidential contenders appear to share this attitude. The proposals that Obama, Clinton, and Edwards put forward would improve our current system rather than scrapping it, using the Massachusetts reform plan as a model. Jonathan Gruber, an MIT economist who helped craft the Massachusetts plan and has consulted with the three candidates on their proposals, told *The Washington Post* that the Democrats have "a sense of realpolitik, of understanding the limitations of what the American voters will go for, while still moving toward the goal of universal coverage."[3] I couldn't agree more.

Imagine, as President Clinton asked lawmakers to do in 1993, looking into the eyes of a sick child who desperately needs medical care and telling that child there is nothing we can do. Or into the face of a woman who has just discovered that her tumor is malignant that her insurance will not cover lifesaving surgery. Or the family forced to sell its home to pay medical bills. More than a decade later, these people and millions more like them exist, spread out over the length and breadth of the country. We can do better. We must do better. We simply can't tolerate this situation any longer.

In his 1945 speech to Congress, President Harry Truman summed up his argument for reform with the following words:

By preventing illness, by assuring access to needed community and personal health services, by promoting medical research, and by protecting our people against the loss caused
by sickness, we shall strengthen our national health, our
national defense, and our economic productivity. We shall
increase the professional and economic opportunities of
our physicians, dentists and nurses. We shall increase the
effectiveness of our hospitals and public health agencies.
We shall bring new security to our people.

Presidents from Johnson to Clinton have made similar ap-
peals in the decades since. We should commit ourselves to
making sure that the next president to utter such words is the
last. The time has come, finally, to fix our broken health-care
system.

Notes

1. The Crisis

1. Kaiser Family Foundation, *The Uninsured: A Primer* (Menlo Park, CA: Kaiser Family Foundation, 2007).

2. Cathy Schoen, Michelle M. Doty, Sara R. Collins, and Alyssa L. Holmgren, "Insured But Not Protected: How Many Adults Are Underinsured? *Health Affairs*, 14 June 2005.

3. Susan Starr Sered and Rushika Fernandopulle, *Uninsured in America: Life & Death in the Land of Opportunity* (Berkeley: University of California Press, 2005), p. 45.

4. Census Bureau, People Without Health Insurance Coverage By Selected Characteristics: 2005 and 2006, http://www.census.gov/hhes/www/hlthins/hlthin06/p60no233_table6.pdf.

5. Robert Pear, "Without Health Benefits, a Good Life Turns Fragile," *The New York Times*, March 5, 2007.

6. Organisation for Economic Co-operation and Development (OECD), *OECD Health Data 2006: Statistics and Indicators for 30 Countries*.

7. Kaiser Family Foundation and Health Research Educational Trust, *Employer Health Benefits 2007 Annual Survey* (Menlo Park, CA: Kaiser Family Foundation, 2007).

8. Sara R. Collins, Karen Davis, Michelle M. Doty, Jennifer L. Kriss, and Alyssa L. Holmgren, *Gaps in Health Insurance: An All-American Problem* (New York: The Commonwealth Fund, April 2006).

9. Testimony of Donna S. Smith before the Commercial and Administrative Law Subcommittee of the House Judiciary Committee, U.S. House of Representatives, July 17, 2007.

10. David U. Himmelstein, Elizabeth Warren, Deborah Thorne, and Steffie Woolhandler, "Illness and Injury as Contributors to Bankruptcy," *Health Affairs* 25, no. 2 (2005): 74–83.

11. David Mechanic, *The Truth About Health Care: Why Reform Is Not Working in America* (New Brunswick: Rutgers University Press, 2006), p. 4.

12. John Abramson, *Overdosed America: The Broken Promise of American Medicine* (New York: HarperCollins Publishers, 2004), p. xii.

13. Richard A. Deyo and Donald L. Patrick, *Hope or Hype: The Obsession with Medical Advances and the High Cost of False Promises* (New York: AMACOM, 2005), p. 14.

14. Ibid., pp. 13–14.

15. Gerald F. Anderson et al., "It's the Prices, Stupid: Why the United States Is So Different from Other Countries," *Health Affairs* 22, no. 3 (2003): 89–105.

16. Marcia Angell, *The Truth About the Drug Companies: How They Deceive Us and What to Do About It* (New York: Random House, 2004).

17. Uwe E. Reinhardt et al., "U.S. Health Spending in an International Context," *Health Affairs* 23, no. 3 (2004): 10–25

18. Steffie Woolhandler, Terry Campbell, David Himmelstein, "Costs of Health Care Administration in the U.S. and Canada," *The New England Journal of Medicine* 349, no. 8 (2003): 768–774.

19. Karen Davis, *The Best Health Care System in the World* (New York: The Commonwealth Fund, March 2007).

20. Michael Sullivan, "Insurance Industry Watches 'Medical Tourism.'" National Public Radio, February 27, 2007.

21. Lucette Lagnado, "Anatomy of a Hospital Bill—Uninsured Patients Often Face Big Markups on Small Items," *The Wall Street Journal*, September 21, 2004, p. B1.

22. Lucette Lagnado, "Twenty Years and Still Paying—Jeanette White Is Long Dead But Her Hospital Bill Lives On," *The Wall Street Journal*, March 13, 2003, p. B1.

23. Henry J. Kaiser Family Foundation/Health Research and Educational Trust, *Employer Health Benefits Survey: 2007* (Menlo Park, CA: KFF/HRET, 2007).

24. "Will Health Benefit Costs Eclipse Profits?" Chart Focus Newsletter, *The McKinsey Quarterly*, September 2004, http://mckinseyquarterly.com/newsletters/chartfocus/2004_09.htm (August 22, 2005).

25. Milt Freudenheim, "Small Businesses' Premiums Soar After Illness," *The New York Times*, May 5, 2007, p. A1.

26. Milt Freudenheim, "New Urgency in Debating Health Care," *The New York Times*, April 6, 2007.

27. Census Bureau, Historic Health Insurance Tables from the Current Population Survey, http://www.census.gov/hhes/www/hlthins/historic/hihistti.html

28. Vern K. Smith and Greg Moody, "Medicaid in 2005: Principles and Proposals for Reform," Health Management Associates (prepared for the National Governors Association), February 2005.

29. Sered and Fernandopulle, *Uninsured in America: Life & Death in the Land of Opportunity*, p. 129.

30. Sara R. Collins, Cathy Schoen, Jennifer L. Kriss, Michelle M. Doty, and Bisundev Mahato, *Rite of Passage? Why Young Adults Become Uninsured and How New Policies Can Help* (New York: The Commonwealth Fund, updated May 24, 2006).

31. David Amsden, "The Young Invincibles," *New York*, April 2, 2007.

32. Sara R. Collins, Michelle M. Doty, Karen Davis et al., *The Affordability Crisis in U.S. Health Care: Findings From The Commonwealth Fund Biennial Health Insurance Survey* (New York: The Commonwealth Fund, March 2004).

33. Ali R. Rahimi, John A. Spertus, Kimberly J. Reid, Susannah M. Bernheim, Harlan M. Krumholz, "Financial Barriers to Health Care and Outcomes After Acute Myocardial Infarction," *Journal of the American Medical Association* 297, no. 10 (March 14, 2007).

34. Jeffrey A. Rhoades and Steven B. Cohen, *The Long-Term Uninsured in America, 2002–2005* (Rockville, MD: U.S. Department of Health and Human Services, Agency for Healthcare Quality and Research, Statistical Brief #183, August 2007).

35. Erik Eckholm, "To Lower Costs, Hospitals Try Free Basic Care for the Uninsured," *The New York Times*, October 25, 2006.

36. Sered and Fernandopulle, *Uninsured in America: Life & Death in the Land of Opportunity*, pp. 105–106.

37. Sara R. Collins, Jennifer L. Kriss, Karen Davis, Michelle M. Doty, and Alyssa L. Holmgren, *Squeezed: Why Rising Exposure to Health Care Costs Threatens the Health and Financial Well-Being of American Families* (New York: The Commonwealth Fund, September 2006).

38. Ibid.

39. Kaiser Family Foundation and Health Research Education Trust, *Employer Health Benefits 2007 Annual Survey* (Menlo Park, CA: Kaiser Family Foundation, 2007).

40. Julie Appleby, "Life in Medicare's Waiting Period," *USA Today*, April 11, 2007.

41. Peter S. Hussey et al., "How Does the Quality of Care Compare in Five Countries?" *Health Affairs* 23, no. 3 (2004): 89–99.

42. Ibid.

43. Elizabeth A. McGlynn et al., "The Quality of Health Care Delivered to Adults in the United States," *The New England Journal of Medicine* 348, no. 26 (2003): 2635–2645.

44. Hussey et al., "How Does the Quality of Care Compare in Five Countries."

45. Ibid.

46. Schoen et al.,"Primary Care and Health System Performance."

47. Ibid.

48. Linda T. Kohn, Janet M. Corrigan, and Molla S. Donaldson, eds., *To Err Is Human: Building a Safer Health Care System* (Washington DC: National Academy Press, 2000).

49. Ibid.

50. Michelle M. Doty and Alyssa L. Holmgren, "Health Care Disconnect: Gaps in Coverage and Care for Minority Adults," Findings from the Commonwealth Fund Biennial Health Insurance Survey, August 2006.

51. Brian. D. Smedley, Adrienne R. Smith, and Alan C. Nelson, eds., *Unequal Treatment: Confronting Racial and Ethnic Disparities in Health Care* (Washington, DC: The National Academies Press, 2002).

52. National Center for Health Statistics, *Health, United States, 2006*, Table 29, http://cdc.gov/nchs/data/hus/hus04trend.pdf#exe.

53. Sered and Fernandopulle, *Uninsured in America: Life & Death in the Land of Opportunity*, p. 158.

54. Ashish K. Jha et al., "Racial Trends in the Use of Major Procedures Among the Elderly," *The New England Journal of Medicine* 353, no. 7 (2005): 683–691.

55. Sered and Fernandopulle, *Uninsured in America: Life & Death in the Land of Opportunity*, p. 158.

56. Final Report of the President's New Freedom Commission on Mental Health, "Achieving the Promise: Transforming Mental Health Care in America," p. 5.

57. J. Walker, E. Pan, J. Johnston, J. Adler-Milstein, D. W. Bates, and B. Middleton, "The Value of Health Care Information Exchange and Interoperability," *Health Affairs*, January 19, 2005, http://content.health affairs.org/cgi/content/full/hlthaff.w5.10/DC1.

58. Institute of Medicine, *Crossing the Quality Chasm: A New Health System for the 21st Century* (Washington, DC: National Academy Press, 2001), p. 15.

59. Juliette Cubanski and Janet Kline, *In Pursuit of Long-Term Care: Ensuring Access, Coverage, Quality* (New York: The Commonwealth Fund, April 2002).

60. Mechanic, *The Truth About Health Care: Why Reform Is Not Working in America*, p. 101.

61. Robert Pear, "Groups Offer Health Plan for Coverage of Uninsured," *The New York Times*, January 19, 2007.

62. Freudenheim, "New Urgency in Debating Health Care."

63. Robin Toner and Janet Elder, "Most Support U.S. Guarantee of Health Care," *The New York Times*, March 2, 2007.

2. THE HISTORY OF HEALTH REFORM

1. Jonathan Cohn, "What's the One Thing Big Business and the Left Have in Common?" *The New York Times Magazine*, April 1, 2007.

2. Jill Quadagno, *One Nation Uninsured: Why the U.S. Has No National Health Insurance* (New York: Oxford University Press, 2005), p. 19.

3. Ibid., page 20.

4. Ibid., page 21.

5. Quoted in ibid., p. 21.

6. Ibid., p. 22.

7. Ibid., p. 23.

8. Cohn, "What's the One Thing Big Business and the Left Have in Common?"

9. Ibid.

10. J. Quadagno, *One Nation Uninsured: Why the U.S. Has No National Health Insurance*, p. 24.

11. Harry S. Truman, *Years of Trial and Hope*, excerpted in *The New York Times*, January 23, 1956.

12. Quoted in J. Quadagno, *One Nation Uninsured: Why the U.S. Has No National Health Insurance*, p. 7.

13. J. Quadagno, *One Nation, Uninsured: Why the U.S. Has No National Health Insurance*, p. 35.

14. Quoted in ibid., page 37.

15. Ibid., p. 13.

16. Ibid., p. 41.

17. Harry S. Truman, *Years of Trial and Hope*, excerpted in *The New York Times*, January 23, 1956.

18. Jennifer Klein, *For All These Rights: Business, Labor, and the Shaping of America's Public-Private Welfare State* (Princeton: Princeton University Press, 2003), p. 5.

19. Malcolm Gladwell, "The Risk Pool: What's Behind Ireland's Economic Miracle and G.M.'s Financial Crisis?" *The New Yorker*, August 28, 2006.

20. Nelson Lichtenstein, *Walter Reuther: The Most Dangerous Man in Detroit* (New York: Basic Books, 1995), p. 289.

21. J. Quadagno, *One Nation Uninsured: Why the U.S. Has No National Health Insurance*, p. 52.

22. Alain C. Enthoven and Victor R. Fuchs, "Employment-Based Health Insurance: Past, Present, and Future," *Health Affairs* 25, no. 6 (2006): 1518–1528.

23. N. Lichtenstein, *Walter Reuther: The Most Dangerous Man in Detroit*, p. 289.

24. J. Quadagno, *One Nation Uninsured: Why the U.S. Has No National Health Insurance*, p. 49.

25. Gladwell, "The Risk Pool: What's Behind Ireland's Economic Miracle and G.M.'s Financial Crisis?"

26. A. C. Enthoven and V. R. Fuchs, "Employment-Based Health Insurance: Past, Present, and Future."

27. J. Quadagno, *One Nation Uninsured: Why the U.S. Has No National Health Insurance*, p. 57.

28. Ibid., p. 64.

29. Ibid., pp. 59–61.

30. Ibid., p. 60.

31. Ibid., p. 67.

32. Ibid.

33. Ibid., p. 68.

34. Ibid., p. 72.

35. Doris Kearns Goodwin, *Lyndon Johnson and the American Dream* (New York: St. Martin's Press, 1976), p. 211.

36. J. Quadagno, "*One Nation Uninsured: Why the U.S. Has No National Health Insurance*," pp. 73–74.

37. D. K. Goodwin, "*Lyndon Johnson and the American Dream*," p. 250.

38. *Public Papers of the Presidents of the United States: Lyndon B. Johnson, 1965.* Volume II, entry 394, pp. 811–815. Washington, D.C.: Government Printing Office, 1966.

39. Ibid. pp. 811–815.

40. J. Quadagno, *One Nation Uninsured: Why the U.S. Has No National Health Insurance*, pp. 96–97.

41. Ibid., pp. 98–99.

42. Ibid., pp. 100–101.

43. Ibid., p. 113.

44. Ibid., p. 115.

45. Ibid., p. 121.

46. Ibid., p. 127.

47. A. C. Enthoven and V. R. Fuchs, "Employment-Based Health Insurance: Past, Present, and Future."

48. J. Quadagno, *One Nation Uninsured: Why the U.S. Has No National Health Insurance*, p. 139.

49. Ibid., p. 139.

50. Ibid., p. 141.

51. Ibid., pp. 141–142.

52. Ibid. p. 144.

53. Ibid., pp. 144–145.

54. Ibid., p. 145.

55. Alain C. Enthoven, *Managed Care: What Went Wrong? Can It Be Fixed?* (The Donald C. Ozmun and Donald B. Ozmun and Family Lecture in Management, the Mayo Clinic, Rochester, MN, November 1999).

56. "A Plausible Revolution in Health," *The New York Times*, October 29, 1991.

57. Marsha R. Gold, "HMOs and Managed Care," *Health Affairs* 10, no. 4 (1991): 189–206.

58. J. Quadagno, *One Nation Uninsured: Why the U.S. Has No National Health Insurance*, pp. 162–164.

59. Theda Skocpol, *Boomerang: Health Care Reform and the Turn Against Government* (New York: W. W. Norton, 1996), p. 25.

60. Paul Starr, "The Middle Class and National Health Reform," *The American Prospect* 2, no. 6 (June 1991).

61. P. Starr, "The Middle Class and National Health Reform."

62. T. Skocpol, *Boomerang: Health Care Reform and the Turn Against Government*, p. 26.

63. Jacob S. Hacker, *The Road to Nowhere: The Genesis of President Clinton's Plan for Health Security* (Princeton: Princeton University Press, 1997), p. 10.

64. Dale Russakoff, "How Wofford Rode Health Care to Washington," *The Washington Post* National Weekly Edition, November 25–December 1, 1991, p. 14, quoted in Skocpol, p. 27.

65. T. Skocpol, *Boomerang: Health Care Reform and the Turn Against Government*, pp. 34–35.

66. Governor Bill Clinton, "Announcement Speech," Old State House, Little Rock, Arkansas, October 3, 1991.

67. T. Skocpol, *Boomerang: Health Care Reform and the Turn Against Government*, p. 39.

68. Ibid., pp. 40–41.

69. "The Health Care System Is Broken; And Here's How to Fix It," *The New York Times*, July 22, 1991.

70. T. Skocpol, *Boomerang: Health Care Reform and the Turn Against Government*, p. 45.

71. Ibid., p. 57.

72. Haynes Johnson and David S. Broder, *The System: The American Way of Politics at the Breaking Point* (Boston: Little, Brown and Company, 1996), p. 113.

73. T. Skocpol, *Boomerang: Health Care Reform and the Turn Against Government*, p. 60.

74. Dana Priest and Kenneth J. Cooper, "Congress Briefed on Health Plan; First Lady Holds Bipartisan Seminar," *The Washington Post*, September 21, 1993, p. A8.

75. H. Johnson and D. S. Broder, *The System: The American Way of Politics at the Breaking Point*, pp. 183–184.

76. Dana Priest, "Consensus Forming on Broad Outlines of How to Fix System," *The Washington Post*, September 16, 1993, p. A14.

77. H. Johnson and D. S. Broder, *The System: The American Way of Politics at the Breaking Point*, p. 188.

78. Ibid., pp. 192–193.

79. Ibid., p. 191.

80. Ibid., p. 229.

81. Starr, "What Happened to Health Care Reform?"

82. Ibid., pp. 198–201.

83. Ibid., pp. 218–219.

84. Ibid., p. 213–214.

85. Ibid., p. 212.

86. Ibid., pp. 220–222.

87. Ibid., p. 213.

88. Starr, "What Happened to Health Care Reform?"

89. "Interest Group Positioning," memorandum from Mike Lux to President Clinton, December 15, 1993, p. 1, quoted in Skocpol, p. 96.

90. T. Skocpol, *Boomerang: Health Care Reform and the Turn Against Government*, p. 103.

91. Ibid., pp. 104–105.

92. Hilary Stout, "Many Don't Realize It's the Clinton Plan They Like," *The Wall Street Journal*, March 10, 1994, p. B1.

93. H. Johnson and D. S. Broder, *The System: The American Way of Politics at the Breaking Point*, p. 528.

94. Ibid., p. 529.

3. WHAT WENT WRONG AND MODELS FOR MAKING IT RIGHT

1. Darrell M. West and Burdette Loomis, *The Sound of Money: How Political Interests Get What They Want* (New York: W.W. Norton, 1999), p. 79, quoted in Quadagno, p. 189.

2. Paul Starr, "What Happened to Health Care Reform?" *The American Prospect* no. 20 (Winter 1995): 20–31.

3. Ibid., p. 112.

4. David Epstein and Sharyn O'Halloran, *Delegating Powers: A Transaction Cost Politics Approach to Policy Making Under Separate Powers* (Cambridge: Cambridge University Press, 1999), pp. 1–3.

5. Wilhelmine Miller, "Value-Based Coverage Policy in the United States and the United Kingdom: Different Paths to a Common Goal," National Health Policy Forum, George Washington University, November 29, 2006, p. 13.

6. Ibid., p. 27.

7. The Henry J. Kaiser Family Foundation, "How Changes in Medical Technology Affect Health Care Costs," March 2007, p. 2.

8. James C. Capretta, "What's Ailing Health Care?" *The New Atlantis*, Spring 2007.

9. G. Harris, B. Carey, and J. Roberts, "Psychiatrists, Troubled Children and Drug Industry's Role," *The New York Times*, May 10, 2007, p. A1.

10. Alex Berenson and Andrew Pollack, "Doctors Reaping Millions For Use of Anemia Drugs," *The New York Times*, May 9, 2007, p. A1.

11. Shannon Brownlee, "The Perils of Prevention," *The New York Times Magazine*, March 16, 2003, p. 52.

12. Capretta, "What's Ailing Health Care?"

13. Victor R. Fuchs, "Health Care Expenditures Reexamined," *Annals of Internal Medicine* 143, no. 1 (July 2005).

14. Institute of Medicine, *Crossing the Quality Chasm: A New Health System for the 21st Century* (Washington, DC: National Academy Press, 2001), p. 3.

15. Ibid., p. 1.

16. National Institute for Health and Clinical Excellence, "A Guide to NICE," April 2005, p. 9. Accessed at http://www.nice.org.uk.

17. Reinhard Busse and Annette Riesberg, *Health Care Systems in Transition: Germany* (Copenhagen: WHO Regional Office for Europe on behalf of the European Observatory on Health Systems and Policies, 2004).

18. Remarks by Chairman Alan Greenspan at the Annual Dinner and

Francis Boyer Lecture of the American Enterprise Institute for Public Policy Research, Washington, D.C., December 5, 1996.

19. Donald F. Kettl, *Leadership at the Fed* (New Haven and London: Yale University Press, 1986, p. 210.

20. Ibid., p. 193.

21. Remarks by Chairman Alan Greenspan, Washington, DC, December 5, 1996.

22. Alan Blinder, "Is Government Too Political?" *Foreign Affairs*, November–December 1997.

4. THE FEDERAL HEALTH BOARD

1. Jane Zhang, "Chronic Condition: Amid Fight for Life, A Victim of Lupus Fights for Insurance," *The Wall Street Journal*, 5 December 2006, p. A1.

2. Cutler, *Your Money or Your Life: Strong Medicine for America's Health Care System*, p. 31.

3. Henry J. Kaiser Family Foundation and Health Research and Educational Trust, *Employer Health Benefits 2006 Annual Survey* (Menlo Park, CA: Kaiser Family Foundation, 2006).

4. Final Report of the President's New Freedom Commission on Mental Health, "Achieving the Promise: Transforming Mental Health Care in America," p. 5.

5. Mary Otto, "For Want of a Dentist: Prince George's Boy Dies After Bacteria from Tooth Spreads to Brain," *The Washington Post*, February 28, 2007, p. B1.

6. Testimony of Dr. Frederick Clark before the Domestic Policy Subcommittee of the House Committee on Oversight and Government Reform, May 2, 2007.

7. Sered and Fernandopulle, *Uninsured in America: Life & Death in the Land of Opportunity*, pp. xvi–xvii.

8. Ibid., p. xxii.

9. Institute of Medicine, *Crossing the Quality Chasm: A New Health System for the 21st Century* (Washington, DC: National Academy Press, 2001), p. 3.

10. Milton Weinstein, "Spending Health Care Dollars Wisely: Can Cost-Effectiveness Analysis Help?" Sixteenth Annual Herbert Lourie Memorial Lecture on Health Policy, No. 30/2005.

11. Institute of Medicine, *Crossing the Quality Chasm: A New Health System for the 21st Century*, p. 17.

12. Ibid.

13. S. R. Collins, K. Davis, M. M. Doty, J. L. Kriss, and A. L. Holmgren, *Gaps in Health Insurance: An All-American Problem*.

14. Susan Starr Sered and Rushika Fernandopulle, *Uninsured in America: Life & Death in the Land of Opportunity* (Berkeley: University of California Press, 2005), pp. 10–11.

15. J. Walker et al., "The Value of Health Care Information Exchange and Interoperability."

16. Stephen C. Schoenbaum, Anne-Marie J. Audet, and Karen Davis, "Obtaining Greater Value From Health Care: The Roles of the U.S. Government," *Health Affairs* 22, no. 6 (November–December 2003): 184.

17. S. C. Schoenbaum, A. J. Audet, and K. Davis, "Obtaining Greater Value From Health Care: The Roles of the U.S. Government," p. 184.

18. Scott S. Greenberger, "Romney Eyes Penalties for Those Lacking Insurance," *The Boston Globe*, June 22, 2005, p. A1.

19. The ideas are similar to those of my colleagues at the Center for American Progress, described in Jeanne M. Lambrew, John D. Podesta, and Terri Shaw, "Change in Challenging Times: A Plan for Extending and Improving the Health System," *Health Affairs*, April 2005, http://content.healthaffairs.org/cgi/content/abstract/hlthaff.w5.119. In addition, they are informed by conversations with numerous experts and practitioners, especially the leadership of the Mayo Clinic, on whose board I serve.

20. David Mechanic, *The Truth About Health Care: Why Reform Is Not Working in America* (New Brunswick: Rutgers University Press, 2006), p. 165.

21. The Commonwealth Fund Health Care Opinion Leaders Survey: Congressional Priorities, January 2007.

22. Sasha Bartolf, "Orszag Discusses New Ways of Alleviating Soaring Health Care Costs," *CQ HealthBeat*, May 22, 2007.

23. Atul Gawande, *Complications: A Surgeon's Notes on an Imperfect Science* (New York: Picador: 2002), p. 236.

24. Ibid., p. 78.

25. Ibid., p. 81.

26. Roger Lowenstein, "The Quality Cure?" *The New York Times Magazine*, March 13, 2005.

27. David M. Cutler, *Your Money or Your Life: Strong Medicine for America's Health Care System* (New York: Oxford University Press, 2004), p. 46.

28. Uwe E. Reinhardt, "The Pricing of U.S. Hospital Services: Chaos Behind a Veil of Secrecy," *Health Affairs* 25, no. 1 (2006): 57–69.

29. Reed Abelson, "In Health Care, Cost Isn't Proof of High Quality," *The New York Times*, June 14, 2007, p. A1.

5. Prospects for Health Reform

1. Kaiser Family Foundation, Health Research and Educational Trust, Employer Health Benefits 2006 Annual Survey. http://www.kff.org/insurance/7527/index.cfm. Accessed June 7, 2007.

2. Business Roundtable Health and Retirement Task Force, "Health Care Costs in America: A Call to Action for Covering the Uninsured," June 2007.

3. House Committee on Veterans' Affairs, "Uninsured Veterans: A Stain on America's Flag" (testimony by Steffie Woolhandler), 110th Cong., 1st sess., June 20, 2007, available online at http://www.pnhp.org/PDF_files/Woolhandler_Veterans_Testimony.pdf.

4. S. R. Collins, K. Davis, M. M. Doty, J. L. Kriss, and A. L. Holmgren, *Gaps in Health Insurance: An All-American Problem.*

5. Len M. Nichols, "Outline of the New America Vision for a 21st Century Health Care System," The New America Foundation, Issue Brief #1, January 2006.

6. Scott S. Greenberger, "Interfaith Leaders Invoke Morality in Healthcare Debate," *The Boston Globe*, December 29, 2005, p. B1.

7. Richard Morin and Shawn Neidorf, "Surge in Support for Social Safety Net: Sympathy for the Poor and Government Aid Programs Returns to 1980s Levels," Pew Research Center for People and the Press, May 2, 2007.

8. David Epstein and Sharyn O'Halloran, *Delegating Powers: A Transaction Cost Politics Approach to Policy Making Under Separate Powers* (Cambridge: Cambridge University Press, 1999), p. 8.

9. Stuart M. Butler, "Building Public Support for Slowing the Growth of Health Care Spending," in *Restoring Fiscal Sanity 2007*, ed. Alice M. Rivlin and Joseph R. Antos (Washington, DC: Brookings Institution Press, 2007), p. 211.

Conclusion

1. Ezekiel Emanuel and Victor R. Fuchs, "Solved!" *The Washington Monthly*, June 2005.

2. Jonathan Cohn, "Uncharitable," *The New York Times Magazine*, December 2004.

3. Perry Bacon Jr., "For Democrats, Pragmatism on Universal Health Care," *The Washington Post*, July 10, 2007, p. A1.

Index